BURBERRY WAR KIT

Service Dress

Pea Jacket

KHAKI UNIFORMS

Designed by Burberrys for the War Office, and proofed by their process.

THE BURBERRY WEATHERPROOF

(Cavalry & Infantry Models)
LORD KITCHENER, referring to THE BURBERRY, described it as "a most valuable addition to his campaigning kit."

Burberry Coats are labelled "Burberrys." Be sure that yours is genuine, otherwise at sorest need the imitation may fail you.

PEA JACKETS

made in Burberry-proofed Regulation Coating, lined camel, fleece, or fur.

BURBERRY WAR KIT

includes, besides full Service dress, Haversacks, Slings, Puttees, Shirts, S.B. Belts, Water Bottles.
Gabardine Ground Sheets and Sleeping Bags.

GABARDINE DAWAC

—a Bivouac only weighing 3¾ lbs. inclusive of pegs

MILITARY BROCHURE POST FREE ON REQUEST

OFFICERS IN FRANCE

can obtain all War Kit from Burberrys' Paris House

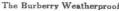

The Burberry Weatherproof

BURBERRYS Haymarket LONDON

also 8 & 10 Boulevard Malesherbes PARIS

BUCKINGHAM PALACE

My message to the Troops of the Expeditionary Force. Aug. 12ᵗʰ 1914.

     •   You are leaving home to fight for the safety and honour of my Empire.

     Belgium, whose country we are pledged to defend, has been attacked and France is about to be invaded by the same powerful foe.

     I have implicit confidence in you my soldiers. Duty is your watchword, and I know your duty will be nobly done.

     I shall follow your every movement with deepest interest and mark with eager satisfaction your daily progress, indeed your welfare will never be absent from my thoughts.

     I pray God to bless you and guard you and bring you back victorious.

An OFFICER'S Manual of the
WESTERN FRONT
1914-1918

Compiled and introduced by Dr Stephen Bull

CONWAY

A Conway Book

First published in 2008 by Conway,
An imprint of Anova Books Ltd
10 Southcombe Street
London W14 0RA
www.anovabooks.com

Compilation and Introduction © Dr Stephen Bull 2008
Volume © Conway 2008

10 9 8 7 6 5 4 3 2 1

A CIP catalogue record for this book is available from the British Library.

ISBN 9781844860722

Printed and bound by WS Bookwell, Finland

Publishers Note.
In this facsimile edition, references to material not included in the selected
extract have been removed to avoid confusion, unless they are an integral part
of a sentence. In these instances the note [not included here] has been added.

*Front cover: A corporal in 'Service Dress' wearing the 1908 pattern web equipment with pack,
carrying the 'Short Magazine Lee Enfield' rifle – the textbook appearance of a British soldier
at the outbreak of the war. From* Infantry Training, *1914.*

Page 1: Sergeant of a Guards regiment in the 'On Guard' position, from Infantry Training,
1914.

Contents

Introduction by Dr Stephen Bull 4

1. Infantry Training, 1914, Chapter X.
   Infantry in Attack, pp.133-147 12

2. Manual of Field Engineering, reprinted 1914,
   Chapter V. Earthworks, pp.24-31..22

3. Notes From the Front, Part 1, 1914,
   Tactical Notes, pp.2-10...46

4. Notes From the Front, Part 3, 1915, pp.10-25 53

5. Trench Standing Orders 1915–16:
   124th Infantry Brigade 67

6. Notes on Minor Enterprises, March 1916 84

7. Notes on the Tactical Employment of Machine
   Guns and Lewis Guns, March 1916, pp.3-19...90

8. Games for Use with Physical Training Tables
   and Training in Bombing, 1916 108

9. Collection of Information Regarding the Enemy, 1915–17 116

10. Instructions for the Training of Platoons for
    Offensive Action, February 1917 117

11. Gas Warfare Monthly Summary of Information,
    No. 15, September 1918 139

Glossary 158

Index 159

INTRODUCTION

The 'Great War' of 1914 to 1918 is frequently described as bloody, stupid, and simple. Bloody it undeniably was: according to official statistics 908,371 British and Empire servicemen died; more than two million were wounded. Almost no family in Britain was untouched. There were campaigns involving British forces in the Middle East, Mediterranean, various parts of Europe, and Africa, but the Western Front proved the great maw of war. Here about three-quarters of British casualties fell, bequeathing to future generations a substantial corner of the French and Belgian landscapes devoted to graves and memorials. There were many thousands of bodies still unrecovered at the time of the Armistice in November 1918 and local farmers were soon being encouraged to report human remains for a five-franc reward. Though many soldiers had no known graves, the neat English garden-style cemeteries still required a force of more than 500 gardeners to tend them.

In certain respects the war was stupid. Some have suggested that the United Kingdom should never have entered the conflict; others that it was vain sacrifice. Conversely, many now think the war was unavoidable, and much more skilfully fought than has generally been acknowledged. Yet even the most dogmatic revisionist would be hard-pressed to state that a struggle so vast and all-encompassing was totally free of error. The necessity for Britain to fight in 1914 remains an active debate, but the war was undeniably a cataclysm that hastened change throughout British society, and led to calls for the end of all war.

The war was never simple. Once started, the struggle between prosperous and populous nations, endowed with industrial strength and great technological virtuosity, could not remain uncomplicated for long. In this respect the popular image of the battleground of the Western Front as tactically stereotypical, with endless, futile, identical charges is wrong. Very quickly professional technicians on all sides came to realise that this war could not be won in the old way – by simple valour of man and horse to the sound of trumpet and drum – but that new ideas and new solutions were needed as a matter of the utmost urgency. The result was scientific and tactical ferment, belied to many observers by both the geographic lack of progress and the military secrecy that shrouded the battlefield. The output of the new was, however, prodigious. In rapid succession there appeared a phalanx of new weapons: specialised small arms; purpose-designed bomber and fighter aircraft; flamethrowers; gas; new shells; ultra long-range and super heavy artillery; new types of mortar and machine gun; and the tank. Less obviously, human organisation and military knowledge was transmuted, often painfully, to make sense of the new world of mechanical and technological destruction now unleashed.

As will become apparent from the following pages no single manual was ever enough to encompass 'modern war', and even before August 1914 numerous publications were required to summarise the military arts. Although examples such as *Field Service Regulations* (priced at one shilling), *Military Cooking, Military Law,* the *Clothing Regulations* and *Care of Barracks* had universal application, each arm of service had several textbooks, and many achieved wide distribution through His Majesty's Stationery Office. For the foot soldier *Infantry Training 1914* and the volumes on musketry were crucial tools of the trade; for the cavalry the key book was *Cavalry Training.* As might be imagined, the technical branches were replete with official instructions. The Royal Engineers covered many different sorts of construction, surveying, drainage, electrics, balloons, railways and signalling, and were expected to undertake siege warfare duties. As such, they boasted a plethora of manuals, though in the context of trench warfare it was arguably *Field Engineering* of 1911 that was of the greatest immediate import. The Royal Artillery had a handbook for virtually every piece of ordnance, plus volumes on ranges, instruments and horse artillery. Sub genres of manual dealt with foreign armies, countries, pay, military history, command, medical and veterinary matters. Officers were instructed to carry the remarkable *Field Service Pocket Book.* The army therefore went to war with perhaps a couple of hundred different types of instruction manual.

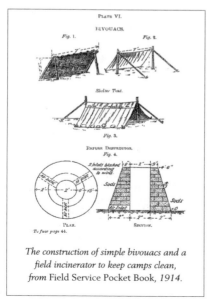

The construction of simple bivouacs and a field incinerator to keep camps clean, from Field Service Pocket Book, *1914.*

Paperwork required its own bureaucracy. A 'Base Stationery Depot' comprising just three officers and seven other ranks accompanied British troops to France in August 1914. The officer in charge was Captain S. G. Partridge, a former War Office clerk, and two other former clerks ranked as Lieutenants. The other personnel were a Sergeant and six expert packers previously employed at the Stationery Office. From these modest beginnings the remit soon expanded far beyond existing manuals, forms, and general office equipment to mass production of printed booklets as well as photographs. Changing role was accompanied by change of title, the humble 'depot' becoming 'Army Printing and Stationery Services'. Some indication of its burgeoning task can be extrapolated from increase in size. Within a year the unit establishment had risen to 20 officers and 176 men. A dedicated press was set up at Havre (Press 'C') in July 1915, with a second at Boulogne in January 1916 (Press 'A'); Abbeville also accommodated a printing section (Press 'B'). Twenty commercial printers in the UK were co-opted to supplement Army efforts. These specialist facilities decreased reliance on the old linotypes of the Royal Engineers and brought into action far more efficient machinery.

Nevertheless early distribution of materials was haphazard, with units being left to request whatever manuals they thought they needed. In perhaps the worst example of muddle, 250,000 copies of the manual *Prevention of Frost Bite or Chilled Feet* were sourced in the winter of 1914–15 and delivered in February, but only 103 of the pamphlets were indented for. That winter over 20,000 men were admitted to hospital with frostbite, and a further 6,500 with 'trench foot': some soldiers were permanently disabled as a result, and 37 died. The timely provision of manuals could not have prevented the problem, but is difficult to believe that education would not have significantly reduced the damage. As a result of fiascos of this nature the system was changed, with Partridge's unit being further expanded and tasked with distribution as well as production and procurement.

By 1918 the 'AP&SS' was of battalion size with over 800 personnel of all ranks, more than half of whom were employed on printing and photographic work. The 'Publications Department' would produce material not only in English, but French, Flemish, various Indian languages and Chinese, as well as volumes for the Americans. Away from the Western Front branches of Army Printing and Stationery were established as far afield as Italy, Greece, Palestine, Egypt, Malta and Mesopotamia. As well as more commonplace manuals, secret documents were printed. These were run off at night, under the supervision of an officer, using judicious division of labour to ensure that none of the men discovered the complete content of the finished publication.

Though working with what was essentially nineteenth-century print technology, metal type, mechanical presses, paper and ink – with distribution by rail, road, and horse – by 1916 speed of production and delivery was swift even by modern standards. Mobile mechanics were able to keep the presses rolling, travelling from job to job on motorcycles. So it was that by the latter stages of the war a 120-page volume detailing an 'order of battle' could be printed and issued in 36 hours. One of the fastest turnarounds was *Precautions Necessary When Firing Rifle Grenades*, the text of which was received at 5.30 p.m. on 15 April 1916. A run of 15,000 finished instructions was complete by morning.

Scales of issue were now used to determine precisely what each unit received, and how frequently, with simple 'field postcards' going to every man in the army, and specialised material being produced in only miniscule print runs. The translation of the German document *Artillery – General Principles* was a short run of just 500. Conversely, manuals such as *Notes from the Front (Part 4)*; *Field Almanac*, 1918; and *Defensive Measures Against Gas Attack*, 1915, were publishers' behemoths with runs of 100,000 or more. The total volumes of paper sent out by AP&SS were massive, and by the last year of war the service was despatching 393,950 separate packets per week. Over 1,100 different items were now held in stock, easily the largest category being manuals and pamphlets of which 750 different titles were produced between 1914 and 1918. Very roughly a new official British manual appeared every 48 hours throughout the war.

Even this veritable flood of official instructional literature was not the whole story, since the stream of words was swollen by many private publications. A commercial trade in non-official military manuals was already established by the Edwardian era, being fuelled by the Volunteer movement and the Boer War. Customers included not only regular officers and a curious public, but from 1908 the re-branded and reorganised part-time 'Territorials'. At Aldershot, the publishers *Gale and Polden* were well placed to become the market leader, but presses all over the country turned out warlike productions as long as stocks of paper held up. London was home to a number of manual printers and publishers. These included W. H. Smith; Forster Croom near Charing Cross; Hugh Rees of Regent Street – the producers of Montague Bates' *Infantry Scout* of 1915, and H. T. Cook of Carter Lane. It was the well-known book publishers John Murray that produced E. J. Solano's splendid 1914 *Field Entrenchments: Spadework for Riflemen*. Some private companies published no more than limited numbers of one or two titles; others large runs. Some canny concerns issued works that were more readable and saleable than manuals, but fulfilled similar needs, as for example United Newspapers who produced Edmund Dane's *Trench Warfare*, and Methuen, the publisher of A. H. Atteridge's *The German Army in War*, both in 1915. Adding these privately sponsored publications to those officially produced brings the total number of manuals to well over a thousand.

Nobody could have found and read every manual: indeed a concerted attempt to do so has lasted rather longer than the war itself. So many publications came forth that for some they became the butt of humour. One story circulated of a booklet entitled *Am I Being Offensive Enough?* – and it is likely that some had to think quite hard before realising that this was a comic spoof. Another version of this joke survives in the pages of the *New Church Times*, a trench newspaper from the Ypres salient. Nevertheless, for many a young officer the avalanche of paper information was the only thing – next to (possibly fatal) experience – that could possibly hope to bring him up to speed in the maelstrom of trench war. Even then, it sometimes seemed that the manuals could never be revised and printed fast enough. As Guy Chapman of 13th Battalion of the Royal Fusiliers explained: 'We had to get our text books by heart before we could impart a crumb of information to our platoons. We seized on and devoured every fragment of practical experience which came

An illustration from the manual that never existed: Questions a Platoon Commander Should Ask Himself, 'Am I being as offensive as I might be ?' Printed in the trench newspaper New Church Times.

our way, gobbled whole the advice contained in those little buff pamphlets entitled *Notes From the Front*, advice, alas! out of date before it was published'.

The objective of this book is to illustrate the variety, demonstrate the scope of subject matter, and show how at least some aspects, such as infantry tactics, changed vastly over four years. Some documents are reproduced in their entirety, others are extracts. The focus is on one theatre only: the Western Front. Although 'other ranks' were often taught from booklets, and indeed created their own précis of manuals during specialised courses, they saw rather less of printed instructions than did officers, and for this reason it is fair to call the entire compendium an 'Officer's Manual'. Artillery and cavalry are mentioned, but the emphasis is the infantry soldier in the trenches.

Chapter 1 is taken from that classic pre-war manual *Infantry Training*, 1914. Its issuance, under the authority of the General Staff – or sale more generally for a consideration of sixpence – came about at least in part due to the recent reorganisation of infantry battalions on a four company system. It reflects state of the art infantry drill and manoeuvres at the outbreak of war. What we see here is what troops were actually expected to do when mounting an attack in battle: a far more complex undertaking, even at this early stage, than many modern pundits would have us believe. Chapter 2, from the *Manual of Field Engineering*,

1911 (reprinted 1914), shows very graphically the sort of thing that attacking troops were up against. Trenches did not appear out of the ether in 1914, but were a planned response to what was hoped to be a temporary defensive requirement.

The important *Notes from the Front* series of booklets produced and distributed in some haste from late 1914 through 1915 are a tangible demonstration that, although operations often failed and casualties were frequently high, British commanders did not simply accept the dire circumstances in which they found themselves. Attempts were made to analyse the almost intractable problems of retirements, highly effective weaponry, and early trench warfare; then to devise new tactics – some of them specifically intended to reduce losses.

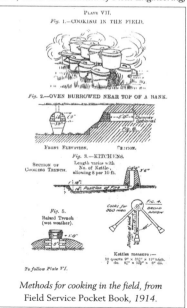

Methods for cooking in the field, from Field Service Pocket Book, *1914.*

Chapters 3 and 4 are drawn from *Notes* Part 1 of 1914, and Part 3 of February 1915. A somewhat jingoistic morale-raising tone stressing the superiority of British troops is apparent, as is reference to the retreat from Mons. Nevertheless much of the advice – on avoiding making an easy target, and holding defensive positions, for example – is extremely useful. Suggestions on the utility of cavalry swords are rather more dubious. Part 3 covers a particularly wide range of subjects – everything from women in espionage and the illegality of the 'unregistered' carrier pigeon, to the role of tight boots in frostbite and the quality of sanitation. Much of this is now quaint nostalgia, but it conceals the grim reality of French or Belgian civilians being taken as spies, and of extremities being amputated after lengthy exposure to water and cold. Part 3 was intended to be issued to 'every officer', and is therefore particularly useful as an indicator of what might be expected throughout the British sector at the time.

Chapter 5 is a complete document being *Trench Standing Orders* for the 124th Infantry Brigade, as prepared by Major E. B. North, Brigade Major. Though undated, internal evidence suggests that it was probably printed in the autumn of 1915 and certainly no later than the beginning of 1916. Its value as a historical document is huge because it is one of the Instructions telling us in detail what a battalion of troops actually did on a daily basis at the front: how they got into the trenches; how they conducted their daily routine; what equipment was to be on hand; what forms were to be filled in; about gas; counter attacks; and what was expected of officers in charge. Possibly the Commanding Officer of the 124th was something of a puritan, for though the issue of rum is mentioned, it is deemed 'undesirable', being only suitable when the men are dismissed after morning 'Stand To'.

Chapter 6, *Notes on Minor Enterprises*, an official publication of March 1916, is a compact gem, a veritable bible of trench raiding and patrolling. Here we learn what raids were for, how to train and prepare, what to wear, and which equipment to carry. Chapter 7 is the main body of the text of *Notes on the Tactical Employment of Machine Guns and Lewis Guns*, also of March 1916. This is significant, illustrating a shift in tactical thinking, brought about at least in part because relatively lightweight 'Lewis guns', often originally regarded as a form of 'automatic rifle', had by this time been widely issued. Machine weapons were no longer to be thought of as static beasts – difficult to deploy and encumbered by water jackets and tripods. Lewis guns were air-cooled, could be handled by one man, and were just about handy enough to accompany the fighting platoons in the forefront of the attack, directly supporting the infantry and providing many a nasty surprise to the enemy. *Notes on the Tactical Employment* marks the stage in the war at which the old, heavy, but long-range and sometimes devastating, Vickers guns were grouped together into the companies of the Machine Gun Corps, while the more nimble Lewis guns became the mainstay of the infantry.

The *Games* manual of September 1916 that makes up Chapter 8 has every appearance of being a silly piece of light relief, considering that it was published midway through the massive attritional battle of the Somme. Yet even this was fun with a serious purpose, for the intention was to produce fit men with quick reactions, and the method of instruction was designed to be highly engaging as well as a change from the potential monotony of traditional 'Physical Training' or 'P.T'. Of all the games 'Bomb ball' is arguably the most interesting, as it consciously aped football for maximum competition value while at the same time developing the skills most necessary for grenade throwing.

The two-page publication, SS 381, *Collection of Information Regarding the Enemy*, in Chapter 9 is particularly intriguing as it shows procedures that were standard for much of the war. German troops frequently carried a good deal of material that was of use in identifying units and assessing morale, and this was a good *aide memoire* as to what to look out for. Diaries, papers, paybooks and maps were fairly obvious sources of intelligence, but even when these were carefully hidden or destroyed marks on clothing and equipment often survived. Personal letters and cards were of more subtle value, for although careful soldiers did not convey their unit or locations in correspondence, mentions of hardship from home, or indications of general attitude, were far more difficult to conceal.

In terms of the development of tactics, *Instructions for the Training of Platoons for Offensive Action* of February 1917, in Chapter 10, was a seminal document, and comparison with *Infantry Training* of 1914 is startling. Perhaps most significant is the fact that it was now thought practicable to treat the platoon as a viable tactical unit in its own right. Where once whole battalions had been armed with rifles, supported by just two – largely immobile – machine guns, now the company, even the platoon, was equipped with a variety of weapons for different tasks. Lewis guns provided close support, and could even lead. Bombers and rifle bombers could deal with invisible targets and clear trenches and bunkers, while riflemen, also equipped with the bayonet, were trained to act in far more flexible ways. Formations, limited in 1914, could now be rapidly changed to meet an unfolding situation, taking advantage of the strengths of the various weapons in the group.

The publication *Gas Warfare: Monthly Summary of Information*, September 1918, in Chapter 11 is illustrative not only of the complexity of gas warfare by the end of the Great War, but of how quickly the manual writers attempted to inform the front line of technological and tactical change. In a period of just four weeks a new gas, a new mask, or a new tactic could enter the fray, and it was the job of the intelligence officer and the Stationery Service to make sure that the latest information was circulated quickly. Not to do so would cost lives. Just how far removed this is from the popular picture of a war in which nothing changed should speak for itself.

Dr Stephen Bull is curator of Military History and Archaeology at the
Museum of Lancashire in Preston.

CHAPTER 1

Infantry Training, 1914
Chapter X. Infantry in Attack.

121. *General considerations.*

1. As is explained in the Field Service Regulations, a commander who decides to take the initiative in forcing a decision usually divides his force into two parts; the first part develops the attack, wears down the enemy's power of resistance by engaging him along his front and endeavouring to force him to use up his reserves, and thus prepares the way for the decisive blow to be struck by the second part, known as the General Reserve. The commander regulates the action of the two parts of his force chiefly by fixing their relative strength and preliminary position, by allotting their respective tasks, and by arranging for the correct timing of their movements in accordance with his general plan of battle.

2. When the commander of an attacking force has issued his orders it lies with the subordinate commanders to distribute the troops at their disposal in accordance with the tasks allotted to them.

Part of the infantry available will form *the firing line*, a portion of which will usually be kept back to form *supports*. Behind these will follow *local reserves* in the hands of battalion, brigade, and divisional commanders.

3. The relative strengths of these bodies will depend on the ground, the information available, time conditions, and the possibility of effecting a surprise. Each portion of the firing line will be given a definite objective or task, and it may also be advisable to fix the limits of its flanks.

4. As much as possible of the line of advance must be reconnoitred beforehand. In close country this will be carried out by officers or scouts; in open country it may be necessary to depend on observation through field glasses. It will usually be found, as a result of such reconnaissance, that certain lines of advance afford better concealment than others, while the localities offering the best facilities for covering fire will be brought to notice.

5. The main essential to success in battle is to close with the enemy, cost what it may. A determined and steady advance lowers the fighting spirit of the enemy and lessens the accuracy of his fire. Hesitation and delay in the attack have the opposite effect. **The object of infantry in attack is therefore to get to**

close quarters as quickly as possible, and the leading lines must not delay the advance by halting to fire until compelled by the enemy to do so.

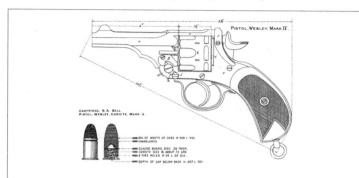

The Webley Mark IV revolver, as depicted in the Dress Regulations for the Officers of the Army, *1900. The Mark IV seen here and the longer barrelled Marks V and VI all saw service in the Great War. Though already an old design in 1914 the .455 round packed a fearsome close-range 'punch'.*

6. **The object of fire in the attack, whether of artillery, machine guns, or infantry, is to bring such a superiority of fire to bear on the enemy as to make the advance to close quarters possible.**

7. The action of infantry in attack must therefore be considered as a constant pressing forward to close with the enemy. Owing to the effect of the enemy's fire, however, this onward movement can rarely be continuous, and when effective ranges are reached there must usually be a fire-fight, more or less prolonged according to circumstances, in order to beat down the fire of the defenders. During this fire-fight the leading lines will be reinforced; and as the enemy's fire is gradually subdued, further progress will be made by bounds from place to place, the movement gathering renewed force at each pause until the enemy can be assaulted with the bayonet.

8. When the ground permits, it is generally necessary to detail special detachments of infantry to provide covering fire for the leading troops. These detachments will usually be detailed from local reserves in the original distribution for the attack, but any commander, at any stage of the fight, may detail troops from those under his command to assist his advance. No fire-unit commander, however, is justified in abandoning, on his own initiative, an advancing *rôle* in order to become a detachment for covering fire.

In undulating or mountainous country it may be possible for these detachments to cover the advance from positions in rear, but in flat country it is impossible for infantry or machine guns to fire over the heads of their own troops, and opportunities for supplying covering fire must be sought on the flanks.

Troops detailed to give covering fire to others must take care to select as targets those bodies of the enemy whose fire is chiefly checking the advance. Great difficulty will often be experienced in detecting which these are, and all ranks must be on the alert to notice any indication of their presence.

As soon as their fire ceases to be effective in aiding the advance of the firing line, it is the duty of troops detailed to give covering fire at once to join in the advance, unless definite orders to the contrary have been received.

9. During the advance, all important tactical points gained, such as suitable buildings, small woods, &c., should, when required, at once be put in a state of defence, so that the enemy may not be able to recapture them and that they may serve as supporting points to the attack. Local reserves will often find opportunities for strengthening localities gained by the firing line, and to assist them in this work, detachments of engineer field companies may be attached to them with advantage.

10. Infantry when advancing must be careful not to interfere with the fire of guns in action. A line of guns should be passed on the flanks, or in the intervals between batteries and brigades. If it is unavoidable that infantry should pass through guns, it should do so at the double. Infantry ceases to mask the fire of artillery about 500 yards in front of the guns on level ground.

11. During the later stages of an attack the replenishment of ammunition in the firing line by individuals will be practically impossible, and all reinforcing troops must be provided with extra rounds for the men in front.

12. When the advancing line is checked by a heavy and accurate fire, it will become necessary to continue the advance by rushes, which, according to the ground and the proximity of the enemy, will be made by the whole line simultaneously or by portions of it alternately.

The length of rushes must depend upon the ground, the enemy's fire, and the physical condition of the troops. It is often advisable to make a rush of some length across open ground in order to reach good cover behind which men can rest. Similarly, if a firing line finds a long downward slope devoid of cover, it is often best to make one rush to the bottom of the slope.

In advancing by rushes within close infantry range the particular portions of the line to move first, and the strength of each such portion, will be determined partly by the ground and the enemy's fire, but chiefly by the **resolution and determination of the various leaders in the front line**. It must therefore be the principal aim of every leader in the front line to get his command forward. Rushes should be as strong as is reasonably possible. Creeping and advancing man by man check the rate of progress and are to be regarded as exceptional methods, only to be employed when it is impossible to gain ground in any other way.

13. Infantry in attack must not delay the advance or diminish the volume of fire by entrenching. Entrenchments in the attack are only used when, owing to further advance being impossible, the efforts of the attacking force must temporarily be limited to holding the ground already won. The advance must be resumed at the first possible moment.

14. Whenever a subordinate artillery commander is allotted a task necessitating co-operation with a certain force of infantry, whether he is placed under the orders of that force or not, it becomes his duty to open communication with its commander, reporting to him in person if possible, in order to obtain full information as to the character of the operation that he is to support, and as to the proposed method of its execution. The best results will be obtained when the artillery commander is able to discuss the situation with the infantry commander before the operation begins, but if this is not possible, or if he cannot remain with the infantry commander, he should be represented by an artillery officer. It is the duty of the infantry commander concerned, once communication with the artillery has been opened, to assist in its maintenance throughout the operation. It is unsafe to rely on one means of communication only, and two, or even more, should usually be arranged.

15. For the purpose of directing the fire of his batteries against what are, for the time being, the most important targets from the infantry point of view, the information which is of primary importance to the artillery commander is the exact positions of the infantry which he is supporting, its immediate objective, and the cause which is preventing it from reaching this objective.

16. Quick-firing guns cannot maintain a rapid fire throughout a battle. Artillery use rapid fire when the infantry firing line is seen to be in need of assistance to enable it to advance; infantry must take every advantage of periods of rapid artillery fire to gain ground.

17. In communications between infantry and artillery the mutual adoption of some system of describing the features of the ground, such as squared maps or panorama sketches, will often save delay and misunderstanding.

18. If the enemy is surprised it is of the utmost importance to increase the demoralization which the surprise will have already produced by pressing forward with the greatest energy. In such conditions the gradual building up, by means of successive reinforcements, of a powerful firing line, should be discarded, and the firing line should be strong from the first. A portion of the attacking force should, however, be retained temporarily in reserve to meet counter-attacks and unforeseen emergencies.

122. *The battalion in attack.*

1. A battalion forming part of the force launched to the attack will be divided by its commander into (1) firing line and supports; (2) local reserve. The relative strengths of these two parts will depend on the task allotted to the battalion and on the ground. When the ground permits a portion of the

battalion will usually be detailed as special detachments to provide covering fire (*see* Sec. **121,** 8).

2. If, owing to the presence of other units on the flanks, a definite frontage as well as an objective is allotted to the battalion, it should be occupied lightly, though not necessarily continuously, from the outset.

3. When more than one company is detailed for firing line and supports it is advisable that each company so detailed should be represented in the firing line from the outset and should have a definite portion of the battalion's objective allotted to it. The maintenance of control and command will thus be facilitated by each company being distributed in depth rather than in breadth, and the inevitable mingling of units will be delayed and reduced.

4. The powers of personal control of a battalion commander upon the field of battle are limited, and success will depend, in a great measure, on the clearness of the order which commits his leading companies to the attack, and the definite objectives which he gives to each company in the original firing line. It is of importance, therefore, that the battalion should not be hurried into action without good reason, but that time should be taken for a survey of the ground, for the issue of orders, and for instructions to be given by company commanders to their subordinates and to the men.

When time permits company commanders and the commander of the machine gun section should be assembled at a point where as much as possible of the ground to be passed over during the operation is visible, and each must be informed, not only of his objective and of what part he is to play, but also of the objectives of the other companies, and those of other portions of the force in their neighbourhood. It will generally be useful to take advantage of this opportunity to point out to rangetakers the objectives of an attack, and to have ranges taken and noted. When the objectives cannot be seen from the spot where the orders are issued, their direction should be stated by reference to a map. Company commanders will act on similar principles in issuing orders to their subordinates.

Occasions will, however, constantly arise in war when instant action is imperative. All commanders and bodies of troops must therefore, when in the neighbourhood of the enemy, be prepared to dispense with preliminaries and to act at a moment's notice.

5. Next to the conception of a sound plan of attack, and the issue of clear and comprehensive orders to the company commanders, the most important duty of a battalion commander is the handling of his local reserve. It is by means of this reserve that he makes his influence felt in action. By providing covering fire by means of special detachments, or by reinforcing the firing line at the right time and at the right place, he keeps the attack moving and eventually attains superiority of fire. But judicious support to the firing line is not all that is required. Not only must its flanks be protected, if exposed, and its advance be supported by fire, but if the enemy is well trained, counter-

attack is to be apprehended, or a sudden reinforcement of the defence may take place when the struggle for fire superiority is at its height. It should be the aim, then, of the battalion commander so to regulate the employment of his local reserve, that while prosecuting the attack with vigour by means of timely reinforcements, he may still have a sufficient force at his disposal to deal with any unexpected developments. He should, therefore, retain at least a portion of the reserve in his own hand as long as possible.

The battalion commander must not, however, fail to throw in reserves at any time when it appears to him necessary to do so during the advance, and in any case, when the moment for decisive action has arrived, every man must be used to complete the enemy's overthrow. Stragglers and slightly wounded men should be collected and formed into reserves whenever met with.

6. The formations in which the local reserve should advance must depend upon the ground and upon the probable effect of the enemy's fire at various ranges. In deciding this question the commander will be guided by the general principles contained in the preceding sections, the object being to get the reserve forward with the least premature expenditure of its fighting energy. The commander of the reserve will, when time permits, take steps to have the ground over which he is to pass reconnoitred before each advance.

7. For the duties of the machine-gun section, *see* Sec. **158,** *et seq* [not included here].

123. *The company in the firing line.*

1. The orders which the company commander will issue before advancing to the attack will be based primarily on those received from his battalion commander, and secondly, on the reports of scouts, on his personal reconnaissance of the ground, and his knowledge of the situation. He should make full use of his horse during the preliminary stages, to reconnoitre ground and to keep in touch with his battalion commander and adjacent companies.

2. The company should, as a rule, be divided into firing line and supports, and, if operating alone, a reserve should be kept in hand as long as circumstances permit.

3. In formulating his orders the company commander should indicate generally the task, objective, and direction of each platoon. If more than one platoon is detailed for the initial firing line, he should allot a definite objective to each. He must arrange for the replenishment of ammunition, and decide on the position of the ammunition animals during the advance. He should inform his officers of the place to which reports are to be sent and of his own position during the earlier stages of the operation.

4. If considered desirable, a few scouts may precede the firing line before fire is opened, to feel the way for the advance. They should be sufficiently far in advance of the firing line and of the exposed flank of the company to obviate surprise and to obtain timely information as to the ground which the

company is to cross. In close or undulating country connecting files may be necessary to maintain touch with the scouts, but they should be recalled as soon as connection can be maintained without them. Scouts preceding the firing line will, when checked, remain in observation until the firing line comes up to them, when they will rejoin their companies. Scouts on the flanks will remain in observation and keep connection with other units on the flanks until recalled.

5. When once the firing line comes under effective fire its further advance will be assisted chiefly by the covering fire of artillery, machine guns, and special detachments of infantry detailed for the purpose, and every advantage of this covering fire must be taken by all attacking troops to gain ground.

6. The various portions of the firing line will also on occasions be able to afford each other mutual support by fire, and all commanders must be on the alert to assist units on their flanks in this manner when the situation requires. Mutual support in the firing line will, as a rule, however, be more automatic than deliberately arranged, and in no case must its employment be allowed to induce hesitation in the advance. The paramount duty of all leaders in the firing line is to get their troops forward, and if every leader is imbued with a determination to close with the enemy he will be unconsciously assisting his neighbour also, for as a rule **the best method of supporting a neighbouring unit is to advance.**

7. The distances between the firing line and supports will be determined by the company commanders, or the officers commanding each portion of the supports, according to the ground; they will seldom be the same in every company, and may vary during the course of an advance. If the ground is favourable supports should close up to the firing line under cover; on open ground the distance between them should be such that the supports will not suffer heavy losses from fire directed at the leading line. The aim of officers commanding supports must be so to handle their commands as to be able to reinforce the firing line with as little delay as possible when required. Care must be taken not to dissipate energy by reinforcing in driblets. Reinforcement should usually be by bodies not smaller than platoons. In the latter stages of an attack it is essential that reinforcing lines should carry up extra ammunition for the men in front.

8. Throughout the action the company commander will maintain communication with his platoon commanders, with the battalion commander, and with the companies on his flanks. He will as a rule accompany the final reinforcement of his company into the firing line.

9. As soon as he has received his orders the platoon commander should explain the situation to his subordinates and point out the line of advance. He must ensure that the movements of his platoon do not mask the fire of units on his flanks, and must endeavour to co-operate with neighbouring units throughout the attack. He must direct the fire of his platoon as long as it is

possible for him to do so, regulate the expenditure of ammunition, and take steps to secure a further supply when required. He must watch the enemy's movements and report at once to the company commander and to neighbouring units if anything of importance is observed; he must also be on the look-out for signals from his company commander and should detail an observer to assist him in this duty. During the advance he must take every opportunity of rallying his command on suitable ground. When the whole platoon is advancing by rushes he must select and point out successive halting places, and must himself lead the rush. After a successful assault he must get the men in his vicinity under control as quickly as possible in preparation for an immediate pursuit.

10. The duty of the section commander is to lead his section. He must see that the direction is maintained, and that he does not mask the fire of neighbouring sections. When the advance is being made by sections, he must select and point out the successive halting places of his section and must regulate the number of men to occupy particular portions of cover. He must control, and when necessary direct the fire of his section, and, as reinforcements come up into the firing line, must take all leaderless men in his neighbourhood under his command, giving them the range and indicating targets. He must pass on quickly all reports that come to him, and inform his platoon commander of any hostile movements which he may observe.

11. All commanders should bear in mind that units are particularly liable to lose direction when moving forward from a hedge or similar feature which lies obliquely to their line of advance.

12. Combined action is always more likely to be successful than isolated effort, and so long as control is possible the individual man must watch his leader and do his best to carry out his intentions. When, however, the section is under heavy fire, section commanders cannot always exercise direct control, and in these circumstances men should endeavour to work in pairs, estimating the range for themselves, firing steadily, and husbanding their ammunition. If incapacitated from advancing, the soldier's first duty is to place his ammunition in a conspicuous place, ready to be picked up by other men, and all ranks must seize opportunities that offer for replenishing their ammunition in this manner.

13. If, when reinforcing the firing line, or at any other time, a soldier loses touch with his section commander, it is his duty to place himself under the orders of the nearest officer or non-commissioned officer, irrespective of the company or battalion to which he may belong.

14. No man is permitted to leave his platoon in action to take wounded to the rear, or for any other purpose, without special orders. After an action any unwounded man who has become separated from his company must rejoin it with the least possible delay.

124. *The assault and pursuit.*

1. The fact that superiority of fire has been obtained will usually be first observed from the firing line; it will be known by the weakening of the enemy's fire, and perhaps by the movements of individuals or groups of men from the enemy's position towards the rear. The impulse for the assault must therefore often come from the firing line, and it is the duty of any commander in the firing line, who sees that the moment for the assault has arrived, to carry it out, and for all other commanders to co-operate.

2. On rarer occasions the commander of the attacking force may be in a position to decide that the time has come to force a decision, and may throw in reinforcements from the rear so that the firing line may gain the necessary impulse for the assault. This will be more likely to occur when the enemy is strong and determined; and the fire fight at close infantry range has been prolonged and severe. In order to ensure an effective and concerted blow it is important that these reinforcements should be brought up well under control, that they should be in sufficient strength to create the necessary impulse, and that all ranks should understand exactly what is required of them.

3. Subordinate commanders in the firing line will decide when bayonets are to be fixed, in accordance with the local conditions of the combat and the nature of the ground. The commander who decides to assault will order the *charge* to be sounded, the call will at once be taken up by all buglers, and all neighbouring units will join in the charge as quickly as possible. During the delivery of the assault the men will cheer, bugles be sounded, and pipes played.

The bursts of artillery fire will have become frequent and intense at this period, the object of the artillery being to demoralize the defenders and reduce their volume of fire. Whether the artillery can continue firing until the assaulting infantry is actually on the point of closing with the enemy, or

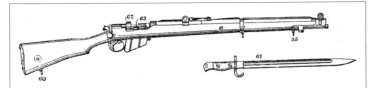

The SMLE – 'Short Magazine Lee Enfield' rifle, standard weapon of the regular infantry and cavalry. The .303 inch 'short' rifle was introduced after the Boer War and was a highly effective military weapon, having a ten round magazine, a reliable bolt mechanism, a handy length, and a fearsome 'sword' bayonet with 17-inch blade much beloved by the drill instructor. From Musketry Regulations, *Part 1, 1909, reprinted with amendments, 1914.*

whether it should increase the range on the first sign of the assault must depend on the slope of the ground.

4. If the assault is successful, and the enemy driven from his position, immediate steps must be taken to get the attacking infantry in hand for the further work that lies before them. The victory is as yet but half won; decisive success will be achieved only by the annihilation of the enemy. A portion of the troops must at once be pushed forward to harry the retreating forces while the remainder are being re-formed, under their own officers if possible, in preparation for a relentless pursuit.

5. Owing to the possibility of hostile gun-fire being brought to bear on the captured position, units should not be re-formed on the position itself, but should move forward to the least exposed localities available. The task of re-forming units will usually fall to subordinate leaders.

6. Steps must be taken to meet a possible counter-attack.

7. As soon as re-formed, units must be ready to carry on the pursuit by day and night without regard to their exhaustion. To sustain a relentless pursuit the utmost energies of every commander must be exerted; only indomitable will can overcome fatigue and carry the men forward. A commander must demand the impossible and not think of sparing his men. Those who fall out must be left behind and must no more stop the pursuit than casualties stopped the assault.

8. Infantry in pursuit should act with the greatest boldness and be prepared to accept risks. Delay for the purpose of detailed reconnaissance or for turning movements is not warranted, and the enemy must be attacked directly he is seen.

The use of 'hasty cover' in the fire-fight. From E. J. Solano's privately produced Field Entrenchments: Spadework for Riflemen, *1914.*

CHAPTER 2

Manual of Field Engineering, Reprinted 1914
Chapter V. Earthworks.

28. GENERAL INSTRUCTIONS.

1. Earthworks may be classed generally under three heads, viz.:—
Trenches, Redoubts, and Gun Emplacements.

Trenches are further distinguished as "fire trenches" or "cover trenches"
according as they are for the firing line or for troops not actually engaged.
"Communication trenches" are excavated covered ways connecting different
parts of a position.

2. The value of concealment cannot be over-estimated, and every effort
must be made to conceal the site of all earthworks in a position. It should be
always borne in mind that invisibility is often as valuable as cover itself, while
one carelessly constructed trench may give the enemy a good idea of the
whole position.

The curves of parapets should be made to assimilate with the natural
contour of the ground. Straight lines and sharp angles are, therefore, out of
place. The fronts of parapets should be carefully covered with sods,
transplanted bushes, &c., to make them resemble their surroundings. Cut
branches become very conspicuous when withered, and if used should be
changed by night.

3. If a parapet is placed on the sky line, spare earth may be piled up
behind the trench and covered with turf, bushes, &c., to make a background
for the defenders' heads, and to conceal its position. As a rule, however, a sky
line is to be avoided. In this connection it must be borne in mind that the sky
line will vary according to the spot from which the position is regarded. As it
is usually most important that trenches, &c., should not be placed on what
would be the sky line to the attacking artillery, the position should, if
possible, be examined, whilst the siting of the trenches is under
consideration, from the positions most likely to be occupied by the attacker's
guns. It is not necessary that entrenchments should be of equal strength
throughout a position. Such portions of the position as are liable to detection

as the result of a distant examination by the enemy should receive earlier and more careful attention than those parts which will not be seen until he has drawn closer.

4. All earthworks, whether completed or not, must be concealed as far as possible, and all tools, materials, and signs of work in progress removed or concealed on each occasion that work proceeding in the presence, or possible presence, of the enemy, is suspended for a longer period than for a routine relief of the working parties.

5. Entrenchments will be used in attack as well as in defence. The main difference between the nature of the works constructed is that in the latter case the position will usually be selected and the work carried out more or less deliberately before fighting begins, while in the former all work will be carried out hastily on ground which may not have been closely reconnoitred beforehand.

6. While the principles of the tactical employment of earthworks must always be borne in mind, the works illustrated in the plates should be regarded as types only and should be varied to suit local conditions, every effort being made to save time, labour and material by utilizing and improving existing cover.

29. Fire Trenches.

1. The ideal site for a trench is one from which the best fire effect can be obtained, in combination with complete concealment of the trench, and of the movements of supports and reserves in rear. Such positions being rarely found, the best compromise must be sought, bearing in mind that a good field of fire up to about 400 yards is of primary importance.

2. When the position includes commanding ground the firing line need not necessarily be on it. The advantage of high ground for a defensive position is often over-estimated. It is, however, desirable that the position should conceal and shelter the defenders' reserves and communications, while enabling the movements of the enemy to be observed.

3. It may sometimes be advisable to place the infantry fire trenches at or near the foot of a slope so as to obtain a grazing fire, while the artillery is posted on higher ground in rear. It must, however, be remembered that it will be difficult, if not impossible, to reinforce the defenders of such trenches, or to supply them with ammunition, water, food, etc., during daylight.

4. Provided the field of fire is good, a parapet cannot be too low, and in some cases no parapet at all need be provided. Every endeavour should be made to arrange the trenches so that the front of one is swept by the fire from those on either hand, for which purpose short trenches up to 40 yards or so in length are more easily adapted to the ground than those of greater length. (Pl. 18.)

Plate 8.

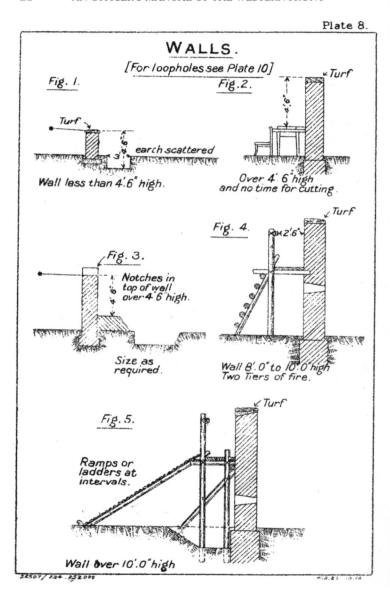

WALLS.

[For loopholes see Plate 10]

Fig. 1.

Turf

earch scattered

Wall less than 4'.6" high.

Fig. 2.

Turf

Over 4'. 6" high and no time for cutting.

Fig. 3.

Notches in top of wall over 4'6" high.

Size as required.

Fig. 4.

Turf

Wall 8'. 0" to 10'. 0" high. Two Tiers of fire.

Fig. 5.

Turf

Ramps or ladders at intervals.

Wall over 10'. 0" high

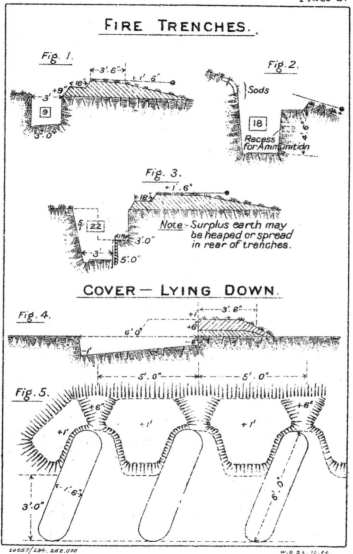

Plate 9.

FIRE TRENCHES.

Fig. 1.

Fig. 2.

Sods

Recess for Ammunition

Fig. 3.

Note.—Surplus earth may be heaped or spread in rear of trenches.

COVER — LYING DOWN.

Fig. 4.

Fig. 5.

Plate 10.

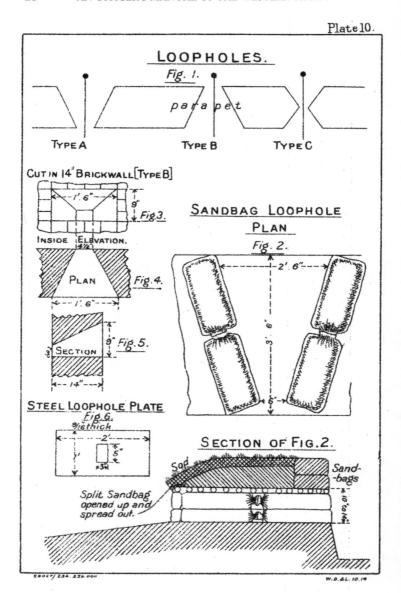

LOOPHOLES.

Fig. 1.

parapet

TYPE A   TYPE B   TYPE C

CUT IN 14" BRICKWALL [TYPE B]

1'. 6"   9"   Fig.3.

INSIDE ELEVATION.   (4½")

PLAN   Fig. 4.

1'. 6"

9"   Fig. 5.

3"   SECTION

14"

SANDBAG LOOPHOLE

PLAN

Fig. 2.

2'. 6"

3'. 6"

6"

6"

STEEL LOOPHOLE PLATE

Fig. 6.

9/16 thick

2'

1'

5"

3"W

SECTION OF FIG. 2.

Sod   Sand-bags

Split Sandbag
opened up and
spread out.

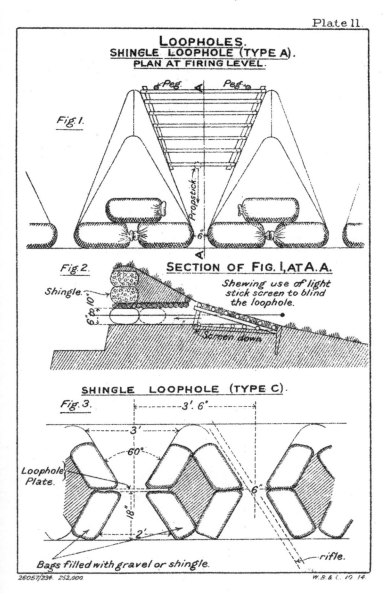

Plate 11.

LOOPHOLES.
SHINGLE LOOPHOLE (TYPE A).
PLAN AT FIRING LEVEL.

Fig. 1.

Peg.   Peg.

Propstick.

6"

Fig. 2.   **SECTION OF FIG. I, AT A.A.**

Shingle.

6" to 10"

Shewing use of light stick screen to blind the loophole.

Screen down.

SHINGLE LOOPHOLE (TYPE C).

Fig. 3.   ------ 3'. 6" ------

------ 3' ------

60°

Loophole Plate.

18"

2'

6"

rifle.

Bags filled with gravel or shingle.

26057/234. 252,000.

W. B. & L. 10 14.

Earth which is not required should be carried away to some spot under cover, or formed into dummy parapets. If wheelbarrows are not available, earth may be carried away in sandbags or in squares of matting, etc., slung to a pole.

5. Every artifice should be used to mislead the enemy as to the positions of the trenches and guns, *e.g.*, conspicuous dummy parapets, not in the alignment of either real fire trenches, or of closely supporting artillery, may be thrown up to draw his fire, and may also be equipped with dummy guns, paper masks, helmets, etc. They would be specially suitable if used in conjunction with a false or advanced position.

Scrub, long grass, etc., forming a natural screen to trenches should not be trampled down or otherwise interfered with more than is absolutely necessary to give a clear field of fire.

6. Turf which may be needed should be taken from some unseen spot, or it may be possible to take it from a strip of ground, which with a little labour may be made to resemble a trench. Turf used for concealing parapets should be laid so that spaces do not occur between adjacent sods.

7. The *design* of a trench will depend on the time and labour available, on the soil, on the site, and on the range and description of fire which may be brought to bear on it, but the following rules are common to all:—

(1) The parapet should be bullet proof at the top.
(2) The parapet and trench should be as inconspicuous as possible.
(3) The interior slope should be as steep as possible.
(4) The trench should usually be wide enough to admit of the passage of a stretcher without interfering with the men firing, and if a step is provided as a banquette, it should not exceed 18 inches in width. (Pl. 9, Fig. 3.)
(5) The interior should be protected, as far as possible, against oblique and enfilade fire, and from reverse fire if there is a danger of fire coming from the rear.
(6) Arrangements for drainage should be made.

8. Types of fire trenches are given in Pl. 9.

To excavate a length of 2 paces per digger of a trench of the type shown in Fig. 1, will take an untrained man about 1½ hours, in moderately easy ground. This does not allow for providing an elbow rest or concealing the parapet.

Should time be available, cover and facility of communication may be much improved by deepening and widening the trench, as shown on Pl. 9, Fig. 3, which allows room for men to pass behind the firing line without disturbing it.

Should a higher command than 1 foot 6 inches be required to enable the defenders to see the ground in front, the parapet must be heightened with earth obtained by widening and deepening the trench. A firing step which should not exceed 1½ feet wide, unless overhead cover is provided, is necessary 4½ feet below the top of the parapet; the interior slope of this step must be revetted.

Pl. 9, Fig. 2, is a case where the ground in front can be seen without any command. For the sake of concealment the excavated earth must be removed or formed into a dummy parapet elsewhere, and the back inside edge of the trench covered up with grass, sods, etc.

9. When entrenching under fire, or in the attack, each man should provide himself with cover as quickly as possible. Pl. 9, Figs. 4 and 5, shows how fairly good cover can be rapidly obtained for individual men lying down. Sods and lumps of earth should be used to revet the inner slope of the parapet. If more time is available the trenches can be improved and deepened as shown by the dotted lines.

In constructing fire trenches in the presence of the enemy, care must be taken to utilize the earth as it is excavated so as gradually to improve the cover provided. It must not be thrown haphazard to the front with a view to subsequent arrangement.

10. An elbow rest is useful because it supports the arm while firing, and is convenient for ammunition, but it is wasteful of head cover, and the vertical exposure of the firer is greater than when no elbow rest is used. It should be 9 inches below the crest and 18 inches wide.

11. Fire trenches should usually be provided with small recesses in which to place packets of ammunition. These will also serve as steps by which to reach the crest, should an advance be ordered. (Pl. 9, Fig. 2.)

12. Ramming earth decreases its resistance to bullets; it should, therefore, be allowed to lie naturally as thrown up, except in the case of shelters constructed under a parapet (Pl. 12, Fig. 3), when some ramming may be advisable to prevent water percolating into them.

30. Entrenching in Frozen Ground.

1. If it is necessary to entrench ground which is frozen, and if there is ample time, the following method will save the heavy labour otherwise required.

A layer of straw 12 to 20 inches thick should be spread so as to rather more than cover the area to be excavated. The straw, having first been covered by a thin layer of earth, is then set on fire at intervals of about 5 yards. The burning should be allowed to go on for 12 hours before the ashes are removed, and digging commences.

2. If water is poured over a parapet constructed during frost its resistance to rifle fire will be increased.

3. The sound of digging in frozen ground can be heard at a distance of about half a mile, while the sparks caused by picks striking stones have been seen up to about 600 yards.

Plate 12.

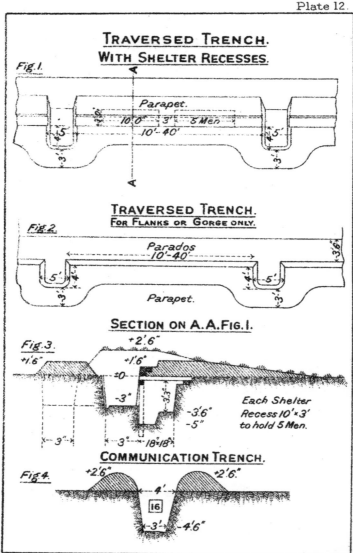

TRAVERSED TRENCH.
WITH SHELTER RECESSES.

Fig. 1.

Parapet.

10.0" — 3' — 5 Men
10'-40'

TRAVERSED TRENCH.
FOR FLANKS OR GORGE ONLY.

Fig. 2.

Parados
10'-40'

Parapet.

SECTION ON A.A. FIG. 1.

Fig. 3.

+2'6"
+1'6"
+1'6"
±0
-3"
-3'3"
-3'6"
-5"
-3"
-3"   18"×18"

Each Shelter
Recess 10'×3'
to hold 5 Men.

COMMUNICATION TRENCH.

Fig. 4.

+2'6"   +2'6"
4'
16
-3'   -4'6"

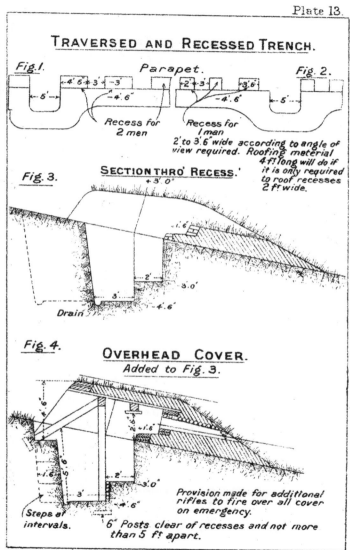

Plate 13.

TRAVERSED AND RECESSED TRENCH.

Fig. 1.   Parapet.   *Fig. 2.*

4' 6" · 3' · 3'   2' · 3' · 3' 6"

5'   4' 6"   4' 6"   5'

Recess for
2 men

Recess for
1 man
2' to 3' 6" wide according to angle of
view required. Roofing material
4 ft. long will do if
it is only required
to roof recesses
2 ft. wide.

Fig. 3.   SECTION THRO' RECESS.
+ 3' 0"

· 1' 6"

2'
3' 0"
3'   3' 0"
4' 6"

Drain

Fig. 4.   OVERHEAD COVER.
Added to Fig. 3.

· 6'

· 1' 6"
2' + 1' 6"

5' 6'
· 1' 6"
2'   3' 0"
3'
4' 6"

Steps at
intervals.

Provision made for additional
rifles to fire over all cover
on emergency.
6" Posts clear of recesses and not more
than 5 ft. apart.

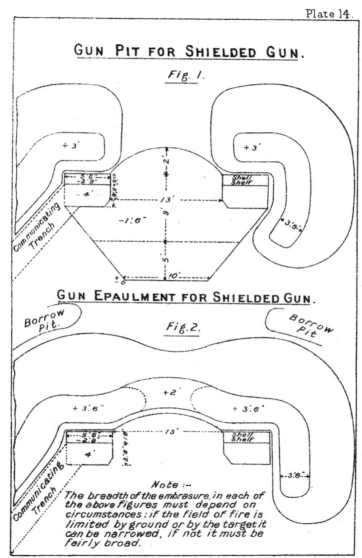

Plate 14.

GUN PIT FOR SHIELDED GUN.

Fig. 1.

GUN EPAULMENT FOR SHIELDED GUN.

Fig. 2.

Note :—
The breadth of the embrasure, in each of the above figures must depend on circumstances; if the field of fire is limited by ground or by the target it can be narrowed, if not it must be fairly broad.

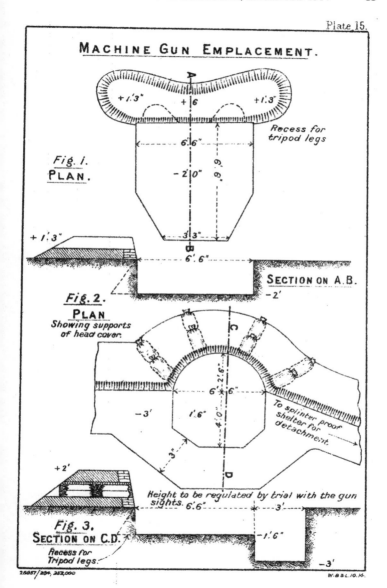

31. LOOPHOLES.

1. Head cover necessitates the provision of some form of loophole or notch but tends to diminish the number of rifles that can be put in line, as well as to reduce the field of fire and view. It generally makes the work more conspicuous, but is of undoubted advantage owing to the feeling of security it inspires, and consequent greater accuracy of fire.

2. Careful arrangement is necessary to ensure the maximum of fire effect and invisibility.

Invisibility is the first consideration during the early stages of the battle and at long ranges, while cover increases in importance as ranges diminish; it may, therefore, occasionally be advisable not to construct head cover at first, but to have materials, such as filled sandbags, ready in the trenches to enable this to be done when further concealment is useless.

3. Loopholes can be made of sandbags, sods, or various other materials such as boxes or sacks filled with earth, or gravel.

The size and shape of the opening must be governed by the extent of ground to be covered by fire, but it will also depend on the width of the parapet, which will vary according to the resisting power of the material used in its construction.

The minimum height of openings for a parapet 3 feet 6 inches thick *on level ground*, using the service rifle at 2,000 yards range, is, for the inside, six inches; for the outside, four inches. The interior height of an earth loophole should seldom be less than 14 inches. This additional allowance is made to enable men to get their heads well forward and under the head cover.

Each loophole must be tested with a rifle, with the bolt removed, to ensure that neither the line of sight nor the line of fire are obstructed.

4. Loopholes should always be blinded by means of a ball of grass, straw or leaves, until they are actually manned. The shadow thrown by the loophole, as well as the hole itself, may be masked by light screens of branches, heather, dry grass, etc. (Pl. 11, Figs. 1 and 2), but it is little use concealing the loopholes if the parapet itself is conspicuous.

5. If the trench is sited for firing downhill, the parapet must be sloped off to the lowest line of fire, before commencing the loopholes. This principle should be equally observed in the case of parapets in elevated positions, or when it is required to fire uphill.

6. Pl. 10, Fig. 1, shows the three types (A, B and C) of loophole which are usually employed.

Loopholes of type A give the defender a good view, and enable him to fire on any point within the angle of opening without moving his position to any great extent. This type of loophole is difficult to conceal and, if covered in, the top sandbags require strong support to prevent them sagging. (Pl. 10, Fig. 2.)

Loopholes of type B are less visible to the enemy, but they are more difficult to observe from and fire through. They are suitable for use in masonry walls, etc. (Pl. 10, Figs. 3 to 5.)

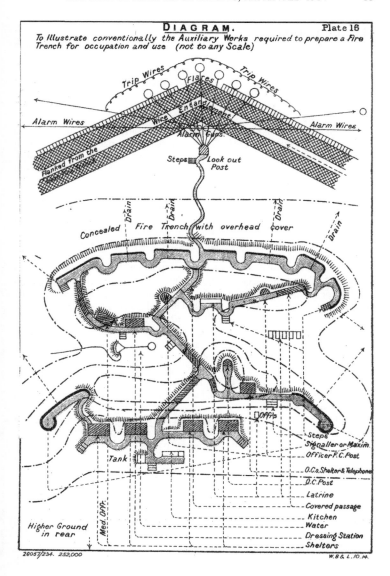

DIAGRAM.
Plate 16

To Illustrate conventionally the Auxiliary Works required to prepare a Fire Trench for occupation and use (not to any Scale)

Trip Wires · Flares · Trip Wires

Alarm Wires · Wire Entanglement · Alarm Wires

Flanked from the ...... · Alarm Guns.

Steps · Look out Post

Concealed Fire Trench with overhead cover

Drain · Drain · Drain · Drain

Higher Ground in rear

Med. Off.

Tank

Offrs

Steps
Signaller or Maxim
Officer F.C. Post
O.C.s Shelter & Telephone
D.C. Post
Latrine
Covered passage
Kitchen
Water
Dressing Station
Shelters

26057/234. 252,000

W. B & L. 10. 14.

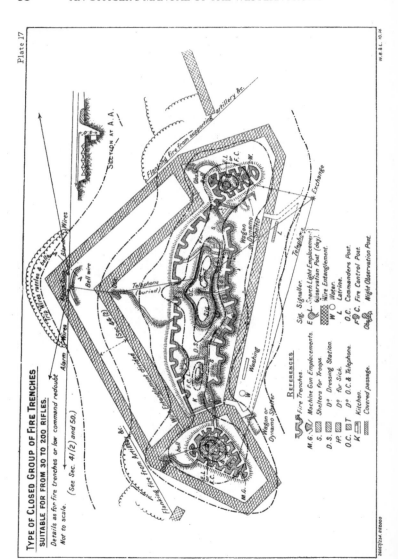

Plate 17.

TYPE OF CLOSED GROUP OF FIRE TRENCHES

SUITABLE FOR FROM 30 TO 200 RIFLES.

Details as for fire trenches or low command redoubt

Not to scale.

(See Sec. 41(2) and 50.)

SECTION AT A.A.

REFERENCES.

Fire Trenches.
M.G. &c. Machine Gun Emplacements.
S. Shelters for Troops.
D.S. D° Dressing Station.
H.P. D° for Sick.
O.C. O.C. & Telephone.
K. T. Kitchen.
Covered passage.
Sig. Signaller.
E. Search Light Emplacement.
Observation Post (day).
Wire Entanglement.
W.O. Water.
L. Latrine.
O.C. Commanders Post.
F.C. Fire Control Post.
Night Observation Post.

Plate 18.

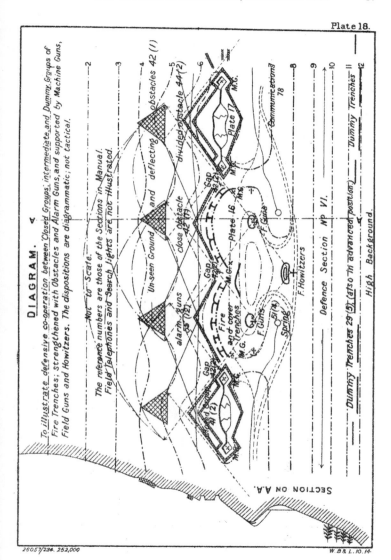

DIAGRAM.

To illustrate defensive co-operation between 'Closed Groups, intermediate and Dummy Groups of Fire Trenches; strengthened with Obstacles and Alarm Guns, and supported by Machine Guns, Field Guns and Howitzers. The dispositions are diagrammatic; not tactical.

Not to Scale.

The reference numbers are those of the Sections in Manual.
Field Telephones and Search lights are not illustrated.

obstacles 42 (1)
and deflecting
dividedobstacle 44 (2)
close obstacle 42 (1)
Unseen Ground
alarm Guns 55 (2)
Fire and cover Trenches
Gap 42 (2)
Gap 42 (2)
Gap 42 (2)
Gap 42 (2)
M.G.
M.G.
M.G.
M.G.
M.G.
Plate 17
Plate 16
Communications 78
F. Guns
F. Guns
F. Howitzers
51 (4)
Spring
51 (4)
Defence Section No VI.
High Background.
Dummy Trenches 29 (5) (also in advanced position)
Dummy Trenches 11
SECTION ON A.A.

2 3 4 5 6 7 8 9 10 11 12

Plate 19.

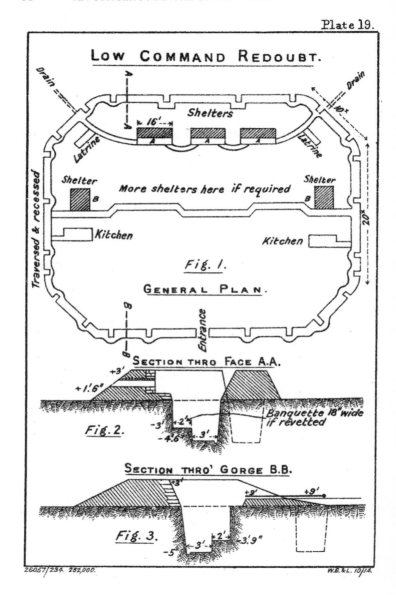

LOW COMMAND REDOUBT.

Drain

Drain

10'

Shelters

16'

A A

A A A

Latrine

Latrine

20'

Traversed & recessed

Shelter

B

More shelters here if required

Shelter

B

Kitchen

Kitchen

Fig. 1.

GENERAL PLAN.

B B

B B

Entrance

SECTION THRO' FACE A.A.

+3'

+1'6"

Banquette 18" wide
if revetted

-3'

+2'

-4'6

-3'

Fig. 2.

SECTION THRO' GORGE B.B.

+3'

+9'

+9'

Fig. 3.

-5'

3'

+2'

3'9"

Loopholes of type C (Pl. 11, Fig. 3) are a compromise between the first two types and can be adapted to give a large field of fire. Thickening the parapet reduces the area round the loophole which can be penetrated by bullets. This is not the case with the first two types.

7. If there is a supply of shingle or gravel available, loopholes may be made as follows:—Place one sandbag inside another, and fill the inner one with the shingle. Three of these double sandbags will make a loophole, and the rest of the headcover can be revetted with single sandbags filled with stones. The sandbags forming the loophole should be placed on edge and stamped or hammered out until the opening is curved as shown, and the bag is about 9'' wide and 6'' high. This loophole requires comparatively few sandbags, and the parapet does not require any extra thickness of earth, while the loopholes can be as close as 3' 3''. (Pl. 11, Figs. 1 and 2.)

8. A form of loophole which has the advantage of giving a wide field of fire and view is a continuous slit along the parapet, except for the supports required for the material above. (Pl. 25, Figs. 2 and 3.)

9. Steel loophole plates are articles of store (Pl. 10, Fig. 6). They may be arranged as shown on Pl. 11, Fig. 3. They make the best head cover, as they are bullet proof, but they would rarely be available for hasty defence work. In the vicinity of railways a strong steel loophole can be made with a string of fish-plates threaded on a rod.

32. DRAINAGE OF TRENCHES.

1. The drainage of trenches must be attended to from the first. The bottom of a trench should be sloped to a gutter, which should preferably be made along the back of the trench. Any water collecting in it should be let off to lower ground, or else into soak pits, which may be about 2 or 3 feet in diameter and 3 feet deep, and filled with large stones. Care must be taken to prevent rain water running into the trenches from the surrounding ground.

33. TRAVERSES.

1. Trenches exposed to enfilade fire and to the oblique fire of artillery, should be traversed and recessed. Traverses give protection against enfilade fire, and also localize the effect of a shell bursting in the trench. (Pl. 12, Figs. 1, 2 and 3.) It is better to make several small traverses than one or two large ones. When the ground is suitable, an irregular line of trench may obviate the construction of traverses, but the best lines of fire must never be sacrificed for this reason. Against oblique or enfilade fire from long ranges, traverses alone will not suffice, on account of the steep angle of descent of the bullets, and overhead cover may be necessary. Recesses in the parapet, large enough to hold one or two men, give protection against such fire, but seriously reduce the number of rifles that can be employed. (Pl. 13, Fig. 1.) Such recesses are best made after the trench has been excavated.

34. COMMUNICATION TRENCHES.

1. If time admits, covered communications must be arranged from the firing line to the rear (Pl. 16). These, by concealing the movements of the defenders, will permit of the firing line being reduced to a minimum in cases where it is being attacked by artillery fire alone, or where the attacking infantry is out of range, and will also enable the supports to reach the firing line under cover. A trench similar to Pl. 12, Fig. 4, will usually suffice.

Time and labour in the construction of these trenches will be economized by a skilful use of the ground and by reducing the distance between the cover for the supports and firing line as much as possible.

They may require parapets on both sides, and where exposed to view or enfilade fire should be traversed and given overhead cover. (Pl. 16.)

2. In positions where their employment as fire trenches might subsequently be desirable, trenches similar to Pl. 9, Fig. 1, may be used.

3. For advancing towards the enemy by means of covered communications leading from the firing line *to the front, see* Mil. Eng., Part II, Secs. 4 and 5 [not included here].

35. COVER TRENCHES.

Cover trenches are useful to protect any men who are not using their rifles. When time is limited and materials are not at hand, a section similar to Pl. 9, Fig. 1, but with slightly higher parapet and no elbow rest, may be employed. If more time and material be available, trenches similar to those shown on Pl. 9, Fig. 3, and Pl. 20, Figs. 1 and 2, should be used.

36. OVERHEAD COVER AND SHELTERS.

1. Overhead cover requires a large amount of material, which will often not be available, and takes a long time to construct. Its main advantage is that it enables the defenders of a trench to continue to use their rifles, even when exposed to a heavy shrapnel fire. Its importance will increase with the progress of aviation and the use of short range grenades and bombs, and its employment in some parts of the firing line may, therefore, be desirable.

2. Overhead cover to keep out splinters of shells, shrapnel bullets and hand grenades, should consist of about 9 to 12 inches of earth, or about 3 inches of shingle, supported on brushwood, boards, corrugated iron, or other materials.

3. In constructing splinter-proof shelters in the firing line it should be recollected that:—

      (*a*) the parapet must not be unduly weakened by them;

      (*b*) they must not curtail the number of rifles available;

      (*c*) it must be possible to get in and out of them quickly;

      (*d*) simple and numerous shelters are better than a few elaborate ones.

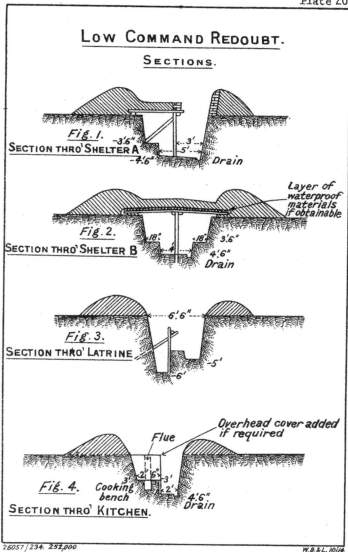

Plate 21

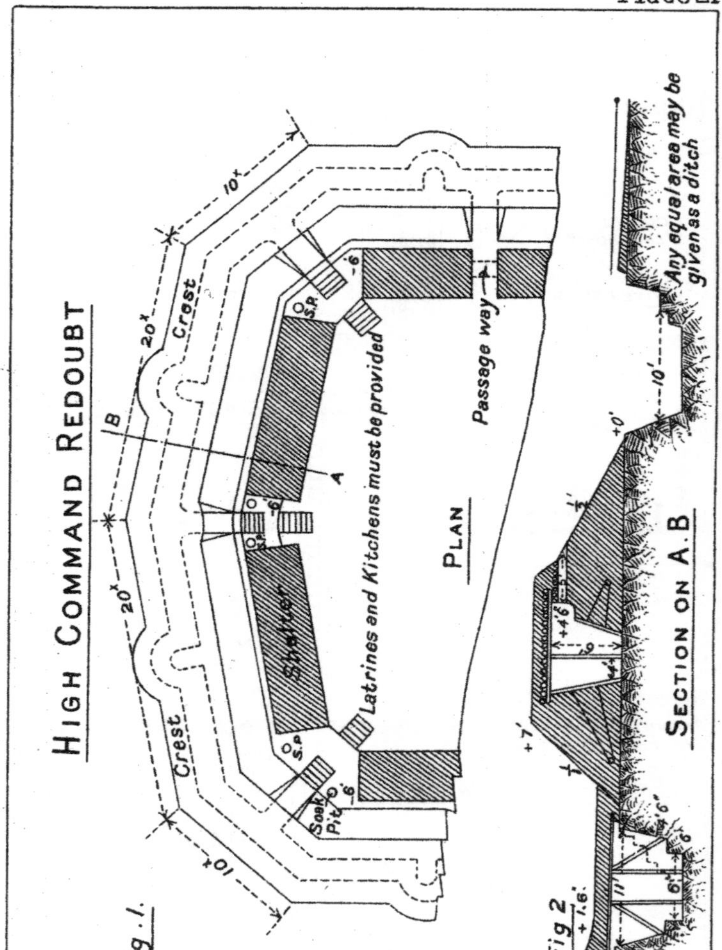

HIGH COMMAND REDOUBT

Fig. 1.

Crest

Crest

Crest

Latrines and Kitchens must be provided

Shelter

PLAN

Passage way

Fig 2

SECTION ON A.B

Any equal area may be given as a ditch

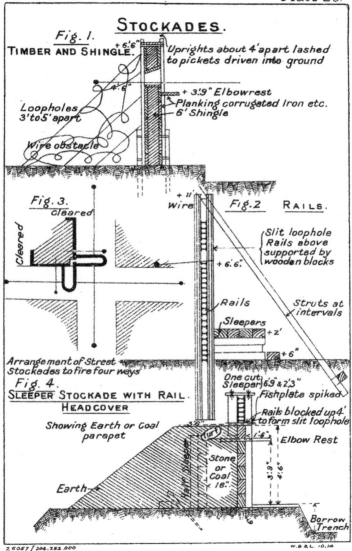

Plate 25.

STOCKADES.

Fig. 1.
TIMBER AND SHINGLE.

+ 6'.6"
+ 4'.6"

Uprights about 4' apart lashed to pickets driven into ground

+ 3'.9" Elbowrest
Planking corrugated Iron etc.
6' Shingle

Loopholes 3' to 5' apart

Wire obstacle

Fig. 3.
cleared

Cleared

Arrangement of Street Stockades to fire four ways

+ 11'
Wire

Fig.2   RAILS.

Slit loophole
Rails above supported by wooden blocks

+ 6'.6"

Rails

Struts at intervals

Sleepers
+ 2'
+ 6'

Fig. 4.
SLEEPER STOCKADE WITH RAIL.
HEAD COVER

Showing Earth or Coal parapet

One cut Sleeper 6'.9" & 2'.3"
Fishplate spiked
Rails blocked up 4' to form slit loophole
Elbow Rest

Stone or Coal 18".

Earth

Half Sleeper

1'.6"
3'.9"
4'.6"

Borrow Trench

2.6057/204.252.000   W.B&L. 10.14

Plate 45.

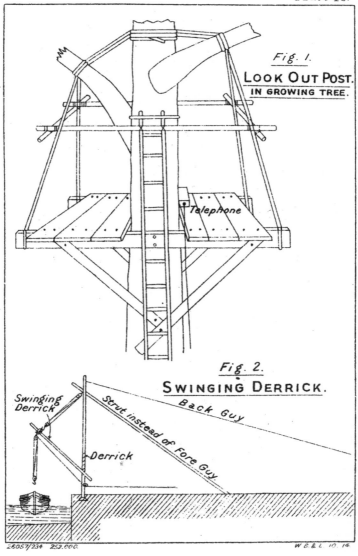

Fig. 1.
LOOK OUT POST.
IN GROWING TREE.

Telephone

Fig. 2.
SWINGING DERRICK.

Back Guy

Swinging Derrick

Strut instead of Fore Guy

Derrick

4. Various forms of splinter-proof shelters are shown on Plates 12, 13, 20 and 21. They all require a great deal of material. They should always be given transverse partitions to localize the effect of shell and be made weather-tight if possible. In firm soil it may be possible to burrow or tunnel shelters in reverse slopes which will suffice without additional materials.

5. In the case of closed works when artillery attack is expected from the front only, splinter-proof shelter for men allotted to the flank defences, may be given in trenches roughly parallel to the front faces. The trenches may be continued with advantage across the whole redoubt, for purposes of communication.

When the artillery attack may come from any direction, shelters for men not firing must be arranged to face in different directions, and parados must be constructed. (Pl. 12, Fig. 3; Pl. 19, Figs. 2 and 3; Pl. 20, Fig. 1.)

6. A roof proof against all except heavy howitzer shell can be made with two layers of rails parallel to the chief line of fire, falling to the rear at a slope of ¼ or steeper, and separated by 1 foot of earth, the top layer being covered with 2 feet of earth.

If timber only is available, the roof may consist of 12 inch logs, with 7 feet of earth above.

7. Where overhead cover is provided arrangements should, if possible, be made for extra rifles to fire over the top of the cover at night or upon emergency. (Pl. 13, Fig. 4.)

37. Protected Look-outs and Observation Posts.

In connection with all fire trenches protected look-outs should, if possible, be provided, which should be indistinguishable from the front. Well-made loop-holes may be sufficient for the purpose. (Pl. 13, Fig. 4.)

Double reflecting mirrors, as provided under Musketry Regns., Pt. II, para. 185, may be usefully employed when obtainable.

Artillery and other commanders will also require observation posts from which to maintain a general control over the fire. Such posts will often be placed clear of all trenches and emplacements, wherever an extensive view is obtainable. The post for sentry group shown on Pl. 30, Fig. 2 [not included here], can be readily adapted to such a purpose, or it may be necessary to provide raised observatories. (Pl. 45, Fig. 1.)

38. Dressing Stations.

Some covered dressing stations should always be prepared in rear of the fire trenches. Each should be large enough to contain a plank table 6ft. 6in. x 2ft. 6in. with 2ft. clear space all round. These stations should be placed near any cover trenches or splinter-proofs that may have been made in order that these may serve as waiting rooms for the wounded, otherwise the communication trenches are liable to become blocked. (Pls. 16 and 17.)

CHAPTER 3

Notes From the Front, Part 1, 1914 Tactical Notes.

Notes from a General Officer at the Front.

(a.) GENERAL.

1. *Defensive positions.*—One of the principal lessons of the war, hitherto, from a tactical point of view, is the necessity for screening positions for defence from the enemy's artillery fire. The enemy's artillery is numerous, powerful and efficient, and our infantry has suffered much from its fire. The German infantry, on the other hand, is inferior to our own in developing fire effect. A short field of fire (500 yards or even less) has been found sufficient to check a German infantry attack. Tactically, therefore, in occupying ground for defence, every effort should be made to combine the fire of our own guns and rifles against the enemy's infantry, while denying to the enemy the use of his artillery by the siting of trenches in positions which it is intended to hold on to, behind rather than on the crest line or forward slopes.

This does not mean that advanced posts have been found to be of no value. On the contrary, in order that full advantage may be taken of the strength of such positions as described above, it has been found essential to prevent the enemy's rapid approach by the use of advance posts supported by the artillery, in order to gain time for deployment and the reconnaissance of the main position, and under favourable conditions for its entrenchment.

2. *Protective troops.*— It was found necessary during the retreat to provide for the protection of a large body of troops such as a corps by means of protective detachments, flank and rear guards, rather than by an outpost line only. We had not been accustomed to handle large bodies of troops in peace time, and in the early days relied entirely on outposts for protection. It was found that the long range and power of the enemy's artillery kept the troops in constant anxiety of being shelled in their bivouacs, and that when pressed by the enemy in retreat the main bodies were easily brought to action and delayed. When protective detachments at a distance from the main bodies were employed, the troops rested in greater security and were able to resume the march confident in the ability of the rear guard to hold the enemy off unless very heavily pressed. These protective detachments at a distance from the main

body have been found to be especially necessary in the absence of protective cavalry. When this system is combined with billeting in depth a march can be resumed at any moment without delay, and mobility is greatly increased.

3. *Passage of rivers.*—Several rivers have been crossed both in advance and in retreat, and experience has been gained both in forcing the passage of a river and in delaying the enemy on a river line. In forcing the passage of a river defended by the enemy's rear guard it may be useful to remind subordinate commanders that there should be no delay in engaging the enemy at the point or points that he is defending and reconnoitring at once for a point of passage which is undefended. Sometimes boats, rafts, a bridge the enemy has forgotten, a weir or other means of crossing have been found. When a sufficient force has been passed over by such means, the enemy, who frequently offers a strong opposition at the defended points, using quite a small force with several machine guns, can be quickly cleared out and a bridge thrown. The Royal Engineers should reconnoitre at once for the most favourable site for a bridge, and can often find and collect materials to supplement the available pontoons. Those with the field companies have twice been found insufficient for the purpose, and the bridging train may not be at hand.

In the event of its being desired to delay the passage of a river by the enemy, it may not be out of place to draw attention to the necessity for studying the bends of the river and the topographical features of the banks, with a view to ascertaining the likely points at which the enemy will try to cross, and making tactical dispositions accordingly. The re-entrant bends towards the enemy should be brought under artillery fire by establishing observation posts from which they can be seen and artillery fire directed upon them. The throwing of a bridge may thus be prevented or it may be destroyed after it has been thrown. Detachments should be posted in advance of any main position that it may be intended to occupy, to prevent the enemy from debouching from the necks of

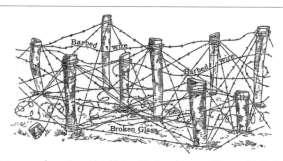

The 'wire entanglement' – with additional broken glass – as illustrated in E. J. Solano's privately produced Field Entrenchments: Spadework for Riflemen, *1914.*

these bends, if he succeeds in crossing. If dispositions of this nature are made with skill the enemy may be delayed for a considerable time, and if desired, time can be gained to prepare a position for defence.

4. *Night operations.*—This corps has not carried out any night attacks, but it has been attacked at night, and it has been found that the enemy apparently makes all his arrangements beforehand and usually advances in strength, dispensing with scouts or advanced parties. No warning is therefore given of his attack and to meet it picquets must be strong and on the position on which they intend to resist. There is no time to rouse them and occupy trenches. If a picquet is watching a road at night, the road should be barricaded and the picquet placed so as to bring fire to bear on the road in front of the barricade, and should never be placed in a position where it can be rushed unprotected by an obstacle.

5. *Formations when on the move.*—It has been found that the long range of the enemy's artillery combined at times with the weakness or even the absence of our own cavalry has rendered the infantry of advanced guards particularly liable to come under artillery fire in close formation. Not only do the troops themselves suffer on these occasions, but the first line transport has been found to be especially vulnerable. It is very undesirable that the march of the main bodies should be delayed by the constant deployment of advanced guards to avoid casualties. It is, therefore, essential, when the front is inadequately covered by cavalry, that troops should be able rapidly to adopt formations suitable when under artillery fire, and they should be trained to adopt these formations as quickly as possible. No more first line transport vehicles than are absolutely necessary should march with an advanced guard, and it has been found desirable to divide first line transport into two echelons.

When troops are fighting, first line transport, first line wagons of artillery, field ambulances and ammunition columns should beware of the deceptive shelter afforded by villages. The enemy's high-explosive shell render villages and the vicinity of buildings especially dangerous. Wounded should not be placed in a church during action. Vehicles and horses should not be crowded together near points that are easily ranged upon by the map, such as barns, haystacks, and road crossings.

6. *March discipline.*—Men who have not been with the colours during the last 4 or 5 years do not understand the necessity for good march discipline. It should be impressed upon all ranks and should be resolutely insisted upon at all training previous to arrival in the theatre of war. There has been straggling, no doubt in great measure due to exhaustion during the first phase, but it is most necessary to tighten up the march discipline again and to prevent undue opening out and straggling.

Horsed wagons should not be parked on the road.

Wagons should never be halted when passing through a village.

When a halt is necessary it should be made before reaching or after passing a village.

Men accompanying trains should carry their rifles and should march in formed bodies.

Each unit should detail an officer with a small party of selected non-commissioned officers and men to march in rear of the unit in order to enforce orders against straggling, leaving the ranks for water, and so forth.

7. *Concealment from aircraft.*—The enemy's aircraft are numerous and efficient, and it is clear that he obtains by this or other means excellent information as to our movements. It has been found impossible to conceal movements of large bodies of troops when on the march from this observation, and the position of large bivouacs can always be observed from the air. But much can be done to conceal artillery positions and trenches, and the use of overhead cover, as we know from our own experience, makes it difficult to ascertain from the air whether trenches and gun emplacements are occupied or not. Troops should therefore be taught to understand the necessity for concealment from aircraft whenever the conditions admit of it

8. *Machine Guns.*—Machine guns have played a very important part in the war, and the enemy is adept in making use of their surprise effect, which has been found to be very great indeed. Till they are located and engaged machine guns play havoc with troops in close order, but when located they are easily knocked out by artillery fire, or silenced by a concentrated rifle fire. Great care should therefore be taken in selecting the positions for machine guns, in occupying them without attracting attention and in reserving fire till a suitable opportunity arrives, in order to make full use of their surprise effect. The only way to avoid the surprise effect of the enemy's machine guns is by careful reconnaissance.

(*b.*) DIVISIONAL MOUNTED TROOPS.

9. *Reconnaissance duties.*—The mounted troops allotted to army corps are strictly limited in numbers and consist of a squadron of cavalry and a cyclist company with each division. Experience has shown that army corps cannot always rely on receiving protection from cavalry, nor can they be sure that information which is essential will be obtained for them by cavalry or even aircraft. In these circumstances there are many duties to be performed by the divisional mounted troops, and if the strictest economy is not employed they will soon become depleted in numbers both from casualties and exhaustion.

No reconnoitring detachment should be stronger than is necessary for its immediate purpose, and no reconnaissance should be sent further afield than is necessary to obtain the actual information required. The greatest care should be taken to limit the scope of these missions and to make instructions clear and definite.

Mounted men should not be kept out at night if it can be avoided.

(*c.*) ARTILLERY.

10. *Tactical handling of.*—Our artillery has suffered from certain

disadvantages during the war so far. In the early battles it was outnumbered, while the ground on the Aisne has prevented its close co-operation with our infantry, which has consequently been exposed to a heavy artillery fire that our guns have been unable to cope with, except with the assistance of aerial observation. The enemy's heavy howitzers have been more numerous than and superior, as regards weight of metal, to our own heavy artillery. The result has been that our infantry have suffered heavy losses from the enemy's artillery fire, and the efforts of our own artillery have necessarily been directed primarily towards neutralizing its effect.

The conclusion has been drawn by some that this should be its primary role. There could be no greater mistake. It should be our constant endeavour to rectify this position and, while developing the power of our artillery, to improve our tactical skill in handling it, so that it is not constantly on the defensive, and so that we may employ its power primarily in attacking the enemy's infantry, and so reverse the situation. As already indicated above the first essential to this end in defence is the skilful use of ground. It is hoped that the Army will soon pass to the offensive and that the artillery will then have an opportunity of showing its ability to support its infantry closely and devotedly in attack. Undoubtedly one of the chief lessons of the war has been the necessity for the closest co-operation between the two arms.

11. *Concealment of.*—Concealment has been forced upon our artillery. The enemy's fire is rapid and accurate, and the effects of the high explosive shell from his heavy howitzers is very damaging, not only to personnel but to material as well. Flashes must be concealed from the front and observation posts selected with the greatest care, and occupied with caution. Emplacements must, whenever possible, be concealed from aerial observation by overhead cover, branches or straw.

12. *Cover for.*—Protection must be provided for the detachments, and, if the situation permits, it is advisable to prepare the emplacements before occupying the position.

13. *Observation by.*—For accurate shooting, effective observation is essential. Forward observation must be used, and for this purpose telephones are invaluable, and great care should be taken of them. Telephone wire should be husbanded.

Visual signalling has been little used.

14. *Co-operation with aircraft.*—Great strides have been made in the co-operation between aircraft and artillery for the purpose of locating hostile trenches and guns and observation of fire. No battery can now be considered really efficient that is not able to range rapidly and accurately by means of aerial observation. The system of coloured lights works well. The new wireless apparatus is better.

15. *Anti-aircraft guns.*—The anti-aircraft gun plays an important part, and if skilfully handled both tactically and as regards shooting should be able to prevent the close reconnaissance of a specified area, or the co-operation of the

enemy's aircraft with his artillery. Efforts should therefore be made to develop the skill of the personnel.

16. *Ammunition.*—The expenditure of 60-pr. And 4.5 howitzer ammunition while on the river Aisne has been very heavy. New formations arriving in the theatre of war should be especially cautioned not to waste ammunition of these natures. In battles of position these weapons are evidently destined to play an important part.

17. *Ammunition columns.*—Roads have often been blocked during operations by ammunition columns. Officers in command of these units should be cautioned to park their horse drawn vehicles off the roads whenever possible.

(*d.*) INFANTRY.

18. *Siting of trenches.*—Owing to the accuracy of the enemy's artillery fire, it is desirable that ground which is to be held defensively or to assist further advance should be entrenched. Trenches should be commenced at once with the light entrenching tool and improved later as opportunity occurs. They should be deep and narrow and should show above the ground level as little as possible, and all trenches should be traversed at intervals of five to ten rifles. When siting trenches it should be borne in mind that the enemy is adept at bringing enfilade artillery fire to bear from flank positions. At any point, such as a salient, at which trenches are particularly liable to this form of fire, great care should be taken as to their siting and they should be especially heavily traversed. Where head cover cannot be provided, cover from shell fire for the troops when not actually using their rifles, can readily be obtained by making recesses in the trenches on the side nearest to the enemy. It has been found that head-cover or anything that in any way interferes with the rapid use of the rifle is a disadvantage in positions where the trenches have a short field of fire and are therefore liable to be rushed. If immunity from shrapnel fire can be obtained up to the moment of having to resist the infantry attack, no more can be hoped for. Communication trenches for supports and ammunition supply are necessary and they should be wide enough to permit of a stretcher being carried along them so as to facilitate the removal of wounded.

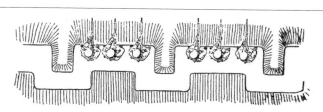

'*Top view of Modern Fire Trench, showing Traverses*', from Edmund Dane's
Trench Warfare, *1915.*

Support trenches may be close to the firing line trenches, but should be so made that the men can lie down and sleep. All trenches must be assimilated to the surroundings.

Elbow rests have not generally been found useful.

Protection against high-explosive shells of howitzers is unobtainable in field operations, but this effect can be localized by traverses.

19. *Observation by aeroplane.*—As soon as it appears that troops have been located by an aeroplane their position should be changed, as it has been found by experience that batteries open fire directly the aeroplane report has been received.

20. *Enemy's ruses.*—The enemy adopts all manner of ruses to deceive our troops such as the use of the white flag, or dressing up in the uniforms of the Allies. It is important therefore that any body of troops approaching our lines should be brought to a halt at some distance from them and one individual only be allowed to advance to establish their *bona fides*. Should they refuse to halt, or act in a suspicious manner, they should, irrespective of their dress or of the circumstances under which they approach, be fired upon without hesitation.

21. *Standing to arms.*—Troops in contact with the enemy should always stand to arms before dawn ready to move off and should remain under arms till the front is reported by patrols to be clear.

22. *Fixing bayonets.*—The enemy's attacks develop so quickly that it is important that troops, and especially protective detachments, should fix bayonets before the final stages are reached. At night, outposts and troops in trenches should have their bayonets permanently fixed. When attacking at night bayonets should always be fixed at the position of deployment.

Extracts from letters received from General Officers at the Front.

Cavalry.—Up to the present long distance reconnaissance by cavalry has been entirely replaced by aeroplanes, the cavalry work being confined to covering the immediate front, or to being massed for operations against a flank. The training of the cavalry with the rifle has been invaluable, and has given them great advantage over the enemy. There have been no cases up to the present of large cavalry charges with the *arme blanche*, but the latter has been used a good deal in small affairs.

Infantry.—The choice of infantry fields of fire is largely governed by the necessity for avoiding exposure to artillery fire. A field of fire of 300 to 500 yards is quite sufficient. This indicates the necessity for accurate shooting at short ranges. Insist on the training of scouts, and particularly on the training of non-commissioned officers as patrol leaders.

An advance should not be made in rigid lines, but with clouds of skirmishers – 5 or 6 yards apart – thrown forward according to the ground and available cover.

The essential thing is to pay attention to the sound principles on which our training has been based.

CHAPTER 4

Notes From the Front, Part 3, 1915

VII.—THE RIFLE AND THE BAYONET.

1. Rapid fire at short ranges is all-important, and the great attention which has been paid to training in rapid fire during recent years has been of the greatest value.

This training must be practised by all concerned to ensure the necessary degree of accuracy combined with rapidity. Rapid charging and recharging of magazines should be constantly practised at all times.

2. It is essential to teach men how to use the bayonet. Unless a man has confidence in his own power to use the bayonet he is unlikely to wish to come to close quarters.

VIII.—CARE OF RIFLES.

A large number of cases have occurred of rifles becoming unserviceable. The following are the principal causes:—

(*a.*) Mud in the lock owing to the rifle being rested on a wet parapet, or dropped on wet ground.

The remedy for this is to cover the bolt with a cloth wrapper or an old sock whenever the rifle is not in use and to place canvas on the parapet. The protecting material can be pulled back when it is required to use the rifle.

(*b.*) Muddy ammunition resulting in mud in the chamber.

The remedy for this is to prohibit ammunition being put on the ground and to provide boxes or tins in which to place the ammunition.

It is a good plan to rub over the ammunition with an oily rag.

(*c.*) Mud in the muzzle owing to rifles being pushed into the sides of trenches.

The only remedy is to see that rifles are clear before firing.

(*d.*) Sticking of cartridges owing to dirt in the chamber or magazine. If the chamber be not kept free from dirt the cartridge case may jam and extraction become difficult. Similarly the magazine must be kept clean and oiled, otherwise the platform will not work freely.

(*e.*) Rust in the lock and insufficient oiling.

A man's life may depend on the care he has taken of his rifle. The bolt and magazine must be tested every day to make sure that they are working freely. If men are never allowed to keep a cartridge in the chamber many accidents will be avoided.

The first duty of a soldier is the care of his arms and no excuse should be accepted for allowing them to become unserviceable.

IX.—REMOVAL OF EQUIPMENT.

The following extract from an order is published for information:—

> Men occupying trenches facing the enemy have been allowed to remove their equipment. Such a practice can only lead, and has already led, to serious consequences.
>
> However trying the circumstances, men must never remove their equipment when in the presence of the enemy, and while on duty in the trenches in the firing line must remain fully equipped.
>
> Packs and haversacks only may be removed at the discretion of commanding officers when the circumstances allow of it.

X.—SITUATION OF HEADQUARTERS.

1. Commanders of all formations must ensure that their headquarters or place to which reports are to be sent are known to all concerned.

This is especially the case where officers command forces composed of several arms.

It is of the highest importance that orders, reports, &c., should arrive promptly. On one occasion it took two officers, two serjeants and eight men three hours to locate an officer commanding a brigade.

2. The Germans make great efforts to locate the headquarters of various formations and as soon as they are located they are shelled. Every effort should therefore be made to reduce the numbers of motors and gallopers going up to headquarters, as its position may thereby be disclosed.

XI.—MAPS OF CAPTURED BRITISH OFFICERS.

Instructions have been issued by the Germans that whenever a British officer is captured, his maps are at once to be taken from him so that he may have no opportunity of destroying them. It has been found that these maps frequently have important information marked on them regarding the dispositions of the British troops. Officers must therefore use every possible means to prevent their maps falling into the hands of the enemy.

This also applies to copies of orders and similar documents likely to prove of value to the enemy.

XII.—AMMUNITION SUPPLY.

1. While the operations were of a mobile nature, as in the cases of the retirement from Mons, the advance up to the battle of the Aisne, or the operations east of Bethune, the normal method of supply as laid down proved satisfactory.

When, however, the operations were of a more stationary character, such as the occupation of the Aisne and the holding of entrenched positions near Ypres, special arrangements were sometimes necessary of which the following is a summary:—

2. A large amount of ammunition was deposited near brigade headquarters which were situated some 500 yards in rear of the centre of the line of trenches held by the brigade. A supply of small arm ammunition was also kept in the trenches of each battalion in boxes distributed among the several companies.

3. The expenditure of ammunition was often considerable, and the headquarters of the brigade were frequently requested to send further supplies to battalions during attacks. On receipt of such messages, men from the reserve carried boxes forward to the firing line, but occasionally small parties from the supports were sent back, and they carried up large numbers of full bandoliers.

4. It was frequently noted that whenever an attack began ammunition was at once demanded, notwithstanding the fact that ample supplies were still in the possession of the firing line.

Each night after dark the small arm ammunition carts brought up fresh supplies from the rear. By day the carts remained some two miles behind under cover.

5. Battalions invariably issued 50 additional rounds per man whenever an engagement appeared probable, and always in the trenches.

A grenade 'bandolier carrier' from Notes From the Front, Part IV, 1915. *The need to carry enough grenades for a 'bombing duel' within a trench system was a problem partly solved by the introduction of various buckets, waistcoats, and harnesses. Nevertheless 'grenadier' or 'bombing' parties of 1915–1917 also included 'spare men' or 'carriers'.*

6. A brigade small arm ammunition reserve was always formed, and was kept supplied by the nearest brigade ammunition column, usually the brigade ammunition column of the Royal Field Artillery brigade, which formed part of the brigade convoys. This brigade reserve kept the battalion small arm ammunition carts fully supplied, usually refilling them each night.

XIII.—SUPPLY SYSTEM.

The following system is reported to work well in the division in which it has been adopted.

For the purpose of supply the division is divided into 6 groups. The composition of the groups varies from time to time, but the following was the normal composition:—

(1.) *Divisional troops* consisting of divisional headquarters, headquarters divisional artillery, headquarters divisional engineers, divisional mounted troops, army veterinary corps, headquarters supply section divisional train, howitzer brigade, heavy batteries, signal company.

(2.) Divisional ammunition column.

(3.) Divisional train (baggage section).

(4.) 1st Infantry brigade group

(5.) 2nd Infantry brigade group

(6.) 3rd Infantry brigade group

Each of these groups consists of infantry brigade headquarters, 4 battalions, 1 field company, 1 field ambulance, 1 brigade field artillery, 1 company divisional train (supply section).

Groups (2) and (3) are dealt with by the divisional troops supply officer, but as they are usually from 8 to 12 miles away from the rest of the division their lorries are loaded at railhead and proceed direct to them.

PROCEDURE AT RAILHEAD, RENDEZVOUS AND REFILLING POINT.

1. *Railhead.*—The supply column is divided into 6 sections to correspond with the 6 groups. A non-commissioned officer is in charge of each section. The supply column supply officer gives to each of these a paper showing the supplies he has to load and this non-commissioned officer gives to the "checker" of each lorry a slip showing the quantity of each commodity that he has to load on to his lorry.

The lorries are then backed up to the railway trucks and loaded.

As soon as the lorries are loaded, and their loads checked, they proceed to the supply column billeting area for the night.

Next day at daylight the supply column proceeds, if the division is marching, to the rendezvous. Should the division be stationary, the groups of the supply column proceed direct to refilling points.

2. *Rendezvous.*—At the Rendezvous the column is met by the senior supply officer, who directs (2) and (3) groups to their units billeting areas, and guides the other four sections to their Refilling Points, which can usually be near to one another, to facilitate supervision.

3. *Refilling Points.*—At these points "dumping" is recommended, as it is found to have advantages over the "tail board to tail board" method, which delays the supply column vehicles unnecessarily.

Different commodities should be "dumped" in separate places, not less than a wagon's length apart, and checked by the supply officer as they are "dumped." The supplies of different groups should be kept far enough apart to prevent the wagons of one group getting in the way of those of another group.

The senior supply officer must satisfy himself that his supplies are correct before the supply column returns to Railhead.

As soon as the supply column has drawn off, the supply sections of the train load up by "groups," and proceed to follow their division if it be on the march, or to distribute to their groups if the division be halted.

The supplies thus loaded on to the supply sections of the train are for use on the following day.

XIV.—Ordnance Supply—Equipment and Clothing.

1. A divisional ordnance officer accompanies each division in the field. This officer sees that the wants of the troops are met as regards ordnance stores and clothing, and he is the medium through whom indents are submitted.

2. Units should keep in touch with this officer, and should keep him informed both as regards their immediate requirements and their probable future requirements.

3. Indents should be put forward at regular intervals, and not delayed until the unit requires a large amount of fresh equipment.

4. All units should be impressed with the necessity of economy as regards stores, and should be made to understand the difficulty of supplying an army in the field, even if nothing more than normal wastage occurs.

5. All surplus and repairable arms and equipment, also captured stores which are worth saving, should be collected by units and handed over to the divisional ordnance officer.

6. The work of divisional ordnance officers will be facilitated if units make their demands on the regulation indent form.

7. On no account should stores be accumulated in units as a provision against probable future wants.

8. Indents for ammunition are unnecessary in the case of units who obtain their supplies through the medium of an ammunition column.

9. Special arrangements exist for the supply of certain stores to army signal units.

10. To each brigade of infantry a warrant officer, Army Ordnance Corps, is attached, who will be found of much assistance to units in arranging for their wants to be met.

11. The system of delivery of stores is as follows:—

(i.) Stores for divisional units are conveyed by lorry by the Army Ordnance Department from Railhead to the Refilling points, where they are transferred to the supply wagons belonging to each unit with the divisional train, this transport being supplemented, if necessary, by the regimental baggage wagons.

(ii.) Units should as far as possible arrange to provide sufficient transport daily to remove all stores from the Refilling point, and a representative of each unit should attend at this point to take over and give a receipt for the stores of his unit.

(iii.) In the case of cavalry divisions, who have no Refilling point, the lorries deliver direct to units in billets, or, when men are in the trenches, to the first line transport vehicles.

(iv.) Stores for corps troops are drawn direct from Railhead by the corps troops supply column.

12. Prompt notice of all changes or pending changes in formations should be given to divisional ordnance officers. This applies more especially to the attachment of corps troops.

13. Units on joining a new formation should, as soon as possible, ascertain that the divisional ordnance officer of that formation is in possession of indents to cover all their outstanding requirements.

14. Any alteration in indents due to casualties or other causes should be at once notified to the divisional ordnance officer.

15. The obtaining of stores by purchase or requisitioning is the duty of the divisional ordnance officer, but when for some particular reason units find it necessary to carry out this duty themselves they must in every case furnish the divisional ordnance officer with a statement of the articles obtained and copies of the receipt notes, a receipt for amounts paid, and a certificate that the articles have been received and are fit for service.

16. Officers requiring equipment or clothing for their personal use, on payment, should send an indent to the ordnance officer of their formation. They will be asked to sign a form authorizing their army agents (or the paymaster paying them) to deduct the value of the articles from their pay.

17. Units should be very careful of entrenching tools in their charge, and this should be impressed on all concerned. It will probably be difficult to replace losses at short notice.

18. Instruction should be given in the assembling and fitting of service harness as early as possible, and in any case before units are warned to prepare for service overseas. Much delay and confusion, both on mobilization and afterwards, will be avoided if this be carried out.

XV.—BILLETING.

The following arrangements have been found suitable, and are published as a guide.

1. The following are suitable compositions for billeting parties:—

(*a.*) *Divisional*—

> Deputy-assistant quartermaster-general.
> Aide-de-camp.
> Staff officers, Royal Artillery and Royal Engineers.
> An interpreter.
> 2 motor cyclists.
> The assistant provost marshal and an officer of the Royal Army Medical Corps should proceed to the headquarters of the billeting area as soon as possible.

(*b.*) *Brigade*—

> Staff Captain with 2 mounted assistants.
> Military mounted police.
> An interpreter.
> An officer, Royal Artillery, with 2 mounted assistants, should accompany the staff captain of an infantry brigade if artillery units are to be billeted in an infantry brigade area. An officer of the Royal Army Medical Corps and the brigade requisitioning officer should join this party as soon as possible.

(*c.*) *Regimental*—

> 1 officer per battalion, an interpreter, and 1 non-commissioned officer per company, with 2 or 3 regimental police.
> 1 officer and non-commissioned officer per battery, field company, Royal Engineers, field ambulance or divisional mounted troops.
> It depends on tactical conditions whether regimental billeting parties can be pushed forward in advance of the fighting troops. Whenever the tactical situation permits they should march in a formed body at the head of their brigades in readiness to move forward. Dismounted men should be mounted on bicycles.

2 (i.) The General Staff fixes generally, according to the tactical situation, the brigade areas, the distribution of troops to those areas, and the general line of protection.

(ii.) Brigade area commanders are responsible for the local protection of their respective areas.

(iii.) The deputy assistant quartermaster-general completes the distribution and fixes the boundaries between areas and units in such detail as may be required, issuing the necessary instructions to the brigade representatives, and, if necessary, assists those representatives to get in touch with the civil authorities.

(iv.) Brigade areas are then sub-divided among the units allotted to the respective areas.

(v.) Officers commanding units similarly distribute their companies, &c., in the sub-areas allotted to them.

(vi.) When the tactical situation permits, infantry should be billeted in villages and mounted troops in the surrounding farms.

(vii.) Sketches of areas should be made whenever possible and handed to units before they arrive in their areas.

3. (i) The position of brigade area headquarters, and when necessary, of outpost headquarters, should usually be fixed by the divisional staff to ensure certainty of intercommunication.

(ii.) If troops arrive in the billeting area before the billeting arrangements are complete, it is important that the leading troops should clear the line of march so as not to block the movement of units who have to pass through to get to their areas.

(iii.) On arrival in their respective areas the troops will not be dismissed from their alarm posts until all measures for security have been taken and the necessary orders issued.

(iv.) All guards and police must be informed of the position of headquarters of their respective units, and must be prepared to direct any officer or messenger to them without hesitation.

(v.) At night representatives of all units in a brigade area must sleep at brigade headquarters and be prepared to deliver orders as required.

(vi.) In each brigade area a signal should be arranged to warn all ranks of the approach of hostile aeroplanes, when troops must take cover.

(vii.) Horses and vehicles must be concealed as far as possible; regular formations must be avoided when horses are picketed or vehicles parked in the open.

(viii.) All approaches to brigade areas should invariably be blocked by an obstacle at night (preferably by wire).

(ix.) If troops are likely to stay in a billeting area for any length of time, a medical officer should be appointed as sanitary officer for that area.

4. *Discipline and control of civil population.*—(i.) On arriving at a town or

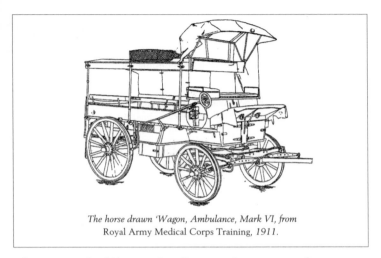

The horse drawn 'Wagon, Ambulance, Mark VI, from
Royal Army Medical Corps Training, *1911.*

village sentries should be posted at all exits until arrangements for protection have been made by the units concerned. Control posts should be established to prevent inhabitants leaving the area or moving in the direction of the enemy.

A sentry who halts a person will not allow him to proceed until he is satisfied that the person is entitled to do so.

The officer or non-commissioned officer posting a sentry must ensure that the sentry understands what are the authorized passes.

(ii.) Divisional orders should be issued as to whether cafés, public houses, &c., are to be allowed to open, and between what hours. Pending the issue of such orders, police should be posted on all such houses.

(iii.) Troops are not to leave their billets without being fully armed and equipped, and only in rare cases (*e.g.*, cooks) should it be necessary for a man to move about even within his billeting area unarmed.

(iv.) A definite time should be laid down by which everyone not on duty is to be in his billet. The hour should, in any case, not be later than 7 p.m.

5. In allotting billets to companies, &c., the following principles should be observed:—

(i.) Headquarters of battalions, &c., must be in a central position and known to all ranks.

(ii.) Each company, &c., must occupy both sides of a street.

(iii.) Officers must be billeted near their men.

(iv.) In allotting accommodation large buildings should be used in preference to small, as supervision, control and food supply are easier; troops can turn out quicker in case of alarm, and chances of sickness or trouble with the inhabitants are minimized.

(v.) Arrangements for water must be notified to all concerned.

(vi.) First line transport should be billeted together.

(vii.) Troops must not use the latrines of the inhabitants. Latrines must, therefore, be dug in suitable places, which must be notified to all concerned.

(viii.) Special precautions must be taken against fire. That is particularly necessary where straw is used for bedding.

(ix.) Cover should be provided for horses whenever possible. It has been found that the average farm in Northern France and Belgium will accommodate at least a half-battery or half-brigade ammunition column.

(x.) Billeting parties should send guides to meet their units, and to conduct 1st line transport and the baggage wagons of the train to their areas.

(xi.) Roads must be kept clear and all transport be moved into yards or fields, or parked clear of traffic space.

(xii.) Before dismissal officers commanding companies, &c., must satisfy themselves that each non-commissioned officer and man under their command understands where his alarm post is, what are the orders in case the alarm is given, and any special orders affecting discipline and interior economy.

(xiii.) All refuse must be burnt or buried under supervision. Burning is preferable, but care should be taken to light fires only in places where the smoke will not disclose the position of troops.

6. The general line to be held by a body of troops and exact points of junction between adjacent units or formations must be clearly defined by the General Staff of the commander of the whole. Thus, in the case of a corps, the line to be held by the corps, and if two divisions are disposed side by side the frontage for which each division is responsible and the point of junction between them, are fixed by the corps headquarters. The same principle must be observed as between brigades in a division and between battalions in a brigade.

XVI.—SANITATION.

1. Strict general cleanliness must be observed in billets, camps, or trenches.

2. Before troops occupy rooms in billets, the latter should be cleared of all unnecessary articles of furniture, &c., and should be thoroughly cleaned.

When troops relieve one another in billets, it should be an established rule that the outgoing unit leaves the billets scrupulously clean and ready for occupation.

(The units arriving from the trenches are usually too exhausted to clean up dirty billets.)

3. All drinking water should be treated with chloride of lime or boiled before being used.

As the water supply is usually liable to contamination by sewage, all drinking water should be obtained from the regimental water carts as far as possible. Empty biscuit tins with wire handles, or camp kettles, should be used for transport and storage. Half a gallon of water per man per day should be provided.

4. Trenches should be provided with latrine seats on the scale of at least two per cent. of the troops occupying them. Urine tins in addition should be provided on the same scale. A removal system should be established, biscuit tins with wire handles being used as receptacles. A plan of a latrine is shown [below].

A.—Latrine buckets (*i.e.*, biscuit tins).

B.—Urine buckets (*i.e.*, biscuit tins) placed on undercut shelf in front wall.

C.—Bar for seat (buried in wall and supported on buried cross-pieces of wood—D).

E.—Back wall scooped out to permit crossing.

F.—Communicating trench 2 feet wide.

X.—Alternative method when removal system is impracticable. Extremity of latrine to be below level of trench, and filled in periodically with earth from Y which later on becomes fresh latrine.

XVII.—Frost-bite.

1. Cold is likely to give rise to frost-bite when the circulation of the blood is impaired.

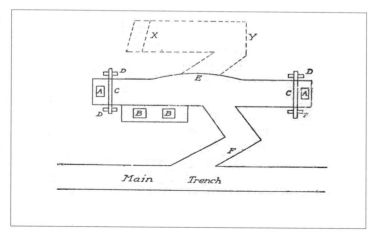

Suggested plan of latrine and urinal for trenches.
(Affords maximum protection for amount of accommodation.)

The feet are likely to be frost-bitten under the following circumstances:—

(*a*.) When the boots and putties are too tight.

(*b*.) When the general circulation throughout the body is less active than normally.

(*c*.) When the socks, boots and putties are wet.

The following precautions should be observed:—

2. Boots should not fit tightly, but should be at least a size too large and loosely laced up. When large boots are worn it is well to wear two pairs of socks; but this is dangerous if the boots are small, as it leads to further pressure on the foot. Putties should never be put on tightly.

3. The best preventive for frost-bite is to take off the boots and dry and rub the feet well; circulation is also improved by moving the toes inside the boot. Greasing the feet or rubbing them with Vaseline, after drying, is also a preventive.

Feet can be kept warmer by wrapping canvas, sacking or other material loosely round the outside of the boot and filling the interval with straw.

4. The general circulation can be kept up by keeping the body warm and dry. A waterproof sheet worn over the great coat is of assistance where no mackintosh is available.

5. A dry pair of socks should be carried in the pocket when available.

6. Officers should see that dry standing is provided in trenches whenever possible, by means of drainage, raising the foot level by fascines of brushwood or straw with boards on top, or by the use of pumps where these are available.

XVIII.—ENEMY'S RUSES.

The enemy makes use of stratagems some of which we should consider dishonourable. The following are instances:—

(*a*.) A party of Germans dressed in French uniforms approached a British outpost and, speaking French, tried to engage them in conversation. At a given signal they attempted to seize the rifles of our men and to overpower them. The attempt was frustrated, but not without loss.

(*b*.) The enemy advanced in the direction of a battalion under cover of a white flag. Instead of surrendering on being approached, they threw down the white flag and forced two companies of this battalion to surrender.

(*c*.) About 20 Germans advanced holding up their hands. Our men came out to accept their surrender when the 20 suddenly lay flat and about 100 other Germans, who had advanced close up unperceived, opened a heavy fire and killed a considerable number of our men before the nature of their action was realized.

(*d.*) The Germans use white armlets to distinguish their own troops in night attacks. Some French troops met German scouts one night with white armlets who represented that they were stretcher bearers searching for wounded. They were allowed to proceed and made a thorough reconnaissance of the French position, after which the enemy delivered a night attack in which the French lost heavily.

(*e.*) Considerable use is made by the enemy of motor cars for reconnaissance. The occupants are dressed as French or English officers and drive boldly through our lines at a great pace. There is reason to believe that motor ambulances have been used for the same purpose.

XIX.—ESPIONAGE.

The following notes dealing with espionage were issued for the guidance of troops:—

1. At Rheims a case occurred where civilians were caught signalling to German troops on the high ground round the town by means of lights, coloured and otherwise, placed at night in windows.

2. Signals have also been sent by intermittent smoke from chimneys.

3. Near Rheims an underground telephone line which was used by a German spy was found connected with the enemy's lines.

4. Several women spies have been caught collecting information regarding names and numbers of regiments, numbers of officers, &c.

5. Spies have been caught at railhead observing entrainment and detrainment of troops.

6. The keeping of unregistered carrier pigeons is illegal, and they are a favourite method of communication by spies. On arrival in a village an order should be given to the Mayor that all cages are to be opened and cellars searched for pigeons. Civilians on the road should also be searched for pigeons, as these latter are sometimes carried in the pocket.

7. An easy means by which spies can approach our lines is in company with refugees. These latter should therefore be questioned by the police, and should not be allowed to enter the area occupied by the troops.

8. Labourers working in the fields between the armies have been detected giving information.

9. People in civilian clothes following our troops when retiring have acted as advanced scouts to German cavalry. A similar procedure may be expected when we are advancing.

10. It is known that German officers and men in plain clothes, or in French or English uniform, have remained in localities evacuated by their armies. French and British stragglers should therefore be handed over to the police.

DIRECTIONS FOR USE & CARE OF TUBE HELMETS.

DESCRIPTION.

These **Helmets** are the same as the "Smoke Helmet" already issued, except that stronger chemicals are added and a "Tube-valve" provided through which to breathe out. The Tube-valve makes helmet cooler and saves the chemicals from being affected by breath.

N.B. Wearer cannot breathe in through the Tube-valve, this is intended for breathing out only.

DIRECTIONS FOR USE.

Remove **Service Cap.** Pull helmet over head. Adjust so that goggles are opposite eyes. Tuck in skirt of helmet under coat collar and button coat so as to close in skirt of helmet. Hold the "Tube" lightly in lips or teeth like stem of pipe, so as to be able to breathe in past it and out through it.

Breathe in through mouth and nose, using the air inside the helmet. Breathe out through tube only.

The valve of the rubber sometimes becomes hard, this can be remedied by breathing out through the valve for about a minute at each helmet inspection, without putting on the helmet.

DIRECTIONS FOR CARE OF TUBE-HELMET.

Never use your Tube-Helmet for practice or drill. Special helmets are kept in each Company for instruction only.

WITHDRAW THESE INSTRUCTIONS FROM THE CASE AND KEEP FOLDED IN YOUR PAY BOOK.

Chemical munitions had been used in a tentative manner earlier in the war, but the massed use of cylinders of chlorine by the Germans in April 1915 marked the unleashing of gas as a 'weapon of mass destruction'. At first Allied countermeasures were amateurish in the extreme, ranging from handkerchiefs dipped in water or urine, to primitive pads across nose and mouth. Not long afterwards came genuine gas masks, initially in the shape of hoods that enveloped the whole head. 'Smoke Helmets', as the first bags were known, were superseded by the 'Tube Helmet'. This is the instruction that accompanied this clammy, sticky, and much reviled object.

CHAPTER 5

Trench Standing Orders, 1915–16 124th Infantry Brigade.

1. RELIEFS.

STANDING ORDERS FOR THE TRENCHES.

(*a*) When a Battalion is taking over a new line of trenches the company and platoon commanders will invariably visit the trenches on the day previous to that on which the relief takes place. They will gain as much information as possible from the company commanders they are relieving.

(*b*) An Officer of each company should proceed in advance to the trenches on the day of the relief to take over, during daylight, all trench stores, ammunition, etc. Mutual receipts for these will be signed.

(*c*) Machine gunners, bombers, snipers and signallers will not be relieved on the same day as companies. They should proceed to the trenches 24 hours before their Battalions, and take over their posts during daylight.

(*d*) The strictest march discipline will be maintained by all parties proceeding to, or from, the trenches. An Officer will march in rear of each company to ensure that it is properly closed up.

(*e*) Reliefs will be carried out as quietly as possible. No smoking or lights will be allowed after reaching a point to be decided on by Battalion Commanders.

(*f*) Guides at the rate of one per platoon, machine gun, or bombing post will invariably be arranged for by Brigade Headquarters when Battalions are being relieved, a similar number of guides will be detailed by them to meet relieving units.

(*g*) On taking over a line of trenches a company commander will at once get in touch with the companies on his right and left; he will ascertain the position of the nearest supporting troops, of the reserve ammunition, of any machine guns or bombing posts, and of his Battalion headquarters; he will ascertain the best and quickest means of obtaining artillery support, and he will have all wires, including the artillery wire if there is one, tested. When his platoons have taken over, and he is satisfied that all is correct, he will inform his Commanding Officer by telephone that the relief of his company is complete.

The Pistol, Signal, Very's Cartridge (Mark II), from the official List of Changes, February 1905. The single-shot Very pistol, used to fire coloured signal flares, sometimes formed part of the officer's equipment at the front.

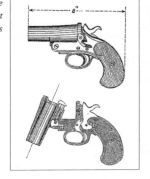

(*h*) The actual relief of trenches should be carried out in the following manner:—

The platoon being relieved gets on the firing step.

The relieving platoon files in behind and halts. On the word "Pass," which will be given quietly, being passed along the relieved and relieving platoons will change places. The Company Commander of the relieving company will then supervise the posting of sentries by his platoon commanders. He will satisfy himself that each post is properly relieved and that the orders for the post are correctly handed over. The greatest care and attention to detail are necessary in this.

The exact frontage for which each platoon commander is responsible will be clearly defined.

Before dismissing his company the Company Commander will ensure that each man has an alarm post from which he can use his rifle freely, and fire at the bottom of our own wire entanglements. Each man must also know the position of company headquarters, the reserve ammunition, and latrines. Every company commander in the front line will have control of the grenadiers employed on his front.

(*i*) Within 24 hours of taking over a new line of trenches a company commander will forward a report on his trenches as follows:—

Garrison of trench.
Field of fire.
Distance from enemy's trench.
General condition of trench.
Whether every man has a post from which he can fire at the bottom of our own wire entanglements.
Number of efficient loopholes.
Whether the parapet is bullet-proof throughout.
Whether sufficient traverses.
State of our wire.
State of enemy's wire.
Drainage.
Number of boxes of reserve ammunition.

Number of bombing posts and of bombs with each.
Number of rounds of **VERY** pistol ammunition.
Number of **VERMOREL** sprayers.
Number of gongs.

A rough sketch showing the position of bombers' posts, machine guns, grenade stores and reserve ammunition should accompany the report.

(*j*) Before handing over trenches, officers commanding companies will draw up a statement containing all available information on the following points:—

Our own trenches and wire.
The enemy's trenches and wire.
Habits of the enemy.
Any part of trench which receives more than ordinary attention from the enemy's guns.
Number of bombing posts and bombs at each.
Number of machine guns on company's front.
Work in hand or contemplated.
What artillery covers the front, and how it is best and quickest obtained.

A list of trench stores, ammunition, &c., will also be drawn up ready for handing over. All stores should be carefully stacked in a convenient place. Ammunition, VERY lights, sandbags, &c., sufficient for at least 24 hours consumption, should invariably be handed over to the relieving unit.

(*k*) The following constitute trench stores and will be handed over on relief:—

S.A.A.	Rifle racks.
Shovels.	Rifle grenade firing stands.
Picks.	Hand grenades.
Loophole plates.	Rifle grenades.
Balers.	VERY pistol cartridges.
Fixed rifle batteries.	Gongs, bells and alarms.
Sniperscope Rifles.	VERMOREL sprayers.
Braziers.	Pumps.
Catapults.	Reserve rations.
Grenade throwers.	

The following will not be handed over:—
VERY pistols.
Pistols, illuminating, 1½ inch.
Telescopic rifles.
Periscopes.
Telephones.

Battalion entrenching tools will not be taken to the trenches. Should the existing tools in the trenches be considered insufficient, application should be made to Brigade Headquarters for a further supply.

2. SENTRIES.

As a general rule the following numbers of sentries will be posted:—

> *By day.*—One sentry for every 3 bays, exclusive of bombers, snipers and machine gunners.

> *By night, in a fog or snowstorm.*—One sentry for each bay, exclusive of bombers and machine gunners.

Sentries will invariably be posted and relieved by a N.C.O. under the orders of the platoon commander.

It must be recognized that no fixed rules can be laid down as regards the number of sentries that are necessary and Battalion Commanders will use their discretion in the matter. The number required will depend on the proximity of the enemy, the tactical situation and, above all, on the state of our own wire entanglements.

3. OFFICER & N.C.O's. OF THE "WATCH."

In every company in the firing line the Company Commander will arrange for his officers to take it in turns to be on "watch" throughout the twenty-four hours.

Likewise in each platoon the Platoon Commander will detail a N.C.O. of the watch.

The Officer and N.C.O's. of the watch will visit all sentries, bombing posts and machine guns within the area of their command once every hour by day and by night.

At night the Officer of the watch will carry a VERY pistol. VERY lights should be used sparingly, as they are often difficult to obtain.

The time when lights are most required is when the Germans are not sending any up.

4. STANDING TO ARMS.

Troops will always stand to arms one hour before daylight and one hour before dark. They will remain under arms in the first instance until the enemy's lines are visible, and in the second instance until darkness comes on. At these hours Company Commanders will arrange for the inspection of arms, ammunition and equipment by Platoon Commanders. The latter will satisfy themselves that each man is in possession of two smoke helmets; ammunition will be made up to 120 rounds per rifle when troops stand to arms.

Whenever men stand to arms Company Commanders will order the parapet to be manned to ensure that every man has a post from which he can fire at the bottom of our own wire.

At the inspection of rifles at the hours of standing to arms Platoon Commanders will satisfy themselves that the bolt action is working freely. A thorough inspection of arms will be held at midday, at which hour men will be washed and shaved.

5. GAS ATTACKS.

(i) It is to be impressed on all ranks that the smoke helmet issued to them affords complete protection against all forms of gas used by the enemy.

(ii) All ranks will invariably carry on their persons two smoke helmets. Instruction is to be given in the method of adjusting smoke helmets rapidly, condemned helmets being used for this purpose.

(iii) Smoke helmets will be inspected at morning and evening "stand to."

(iv) The direction of the wind will be studied and special precautions taken when it favours a gas attack by the enemy.

(v) On the first sign of gas, whether it is detected by sight or smell, the sentries will sound the alarm gongs and bells which are hung up at intervals throughout the trenches. On hearing this alarm every officer and man will at once adjust his smoke helmet and fall in on his alarm post. Nobody will remain in dug-outs. To make certain of the warning reaching everybody, the order "Put on smoke helmets" will be passed from man to man throughout the trenches held by the Division.

(vi) The officers in command of the trenches opposite the section of the enemy's line from which the gas is proceeding will send the S.O.S. call to the artillery, and will order rapid fire to be opened on the enemy trenches. Neighbouring sectors of defence will be at once warned.

(vii) When the gas cloud is sufficiently thick to hide the enemy's front parapets, machine guns and rifles will open fire in short bursts on fixed lines covering the enemy's trenches, in order to inflict casualties, pierce gas tubes, and break up the density of the enemy's gas cloud.

(viii) Garrisons of trenches on the flanks of the front threatened will be prepared to open a flanking fire on the enemy should he attempt to advance from his front line.

(ix) As soon as the S.O.S. call has been sent to the artillery, messages will be sent to Brigade H.Q. and the artillery "gas trench (es)................"

(x) Rifle bolts and machine-gun crank handles to be worked backwards and forwards while gas is about, to prevent the gas impairing the action.

(xi) Vermoral sprayers to be used in trenches and dug-outs in the affected area as soon as the gas has passed over, in order that gas helmets may be taken off.

(xii) Measures will be taken to prevent stragglers.

6. FIXING OF BAYONETS.

Bayonets will always be fixed during the hours of darkness, during a snowstorm, or thick mist, or when the proximity of the enemy renders this course advisable.

7. COUNTER-ATTACKS.

As soon as possible after taking over a new line, Battalion Commanders will draw up and submit to Brigade Headquarters their scheme for counter-attacking the enemy should he gain possession of any part of their line.

In framing this scheme it must be borne in mind that in every line of trenches there are certain points which would be of value to the enemy if captured by him, whereas there are others which would be of little use to him.

Should the enemy attack and occupy any portion of our trenches he will be immediately counter-attacked and driven out by the nearest body of troops. All ranks must clearly understand that counter-attacks made at once and without hesitation will usually be successful, even if made by small numbers, but that a counter-attack, once the enemy has been given time to establish himself, is a very difficult and costly operation.

Troops counter-attacking must themselves keep back a small reserve. It often happens that though the counter-attack as a whole is successful small

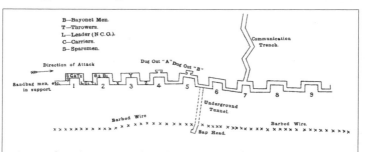

Diagram from The Training and Employment of Grenadiers, *1915. This shows the latest tactics by means of which a 'grenadier party' worked its way down a trench throwing grenades ahead of them. 'Bayonet men' in the lead were followed by dedicated 'throwers' and 'carriers'.*

groups of the enemy are able to establish themselves in buildings or behind other cover and fire into the backs of the counter-attacking troops after they have passed. The reserve is designed to deal with these and must do so instantly or the success of the counter-attack may be endangered. Unless specially ordered to the contrary troops counter-attacking will not go beyond our own original fire trenches, which they will re-occupy and hold. If required for some special reason to go beyond those trenches the objective must be clearly explained to all troops, and they are on no account to go beyond that objective.

This principle is equally applicable to the action of the reserve of the counter-attack, who, as soon as their object is achieved, must be prepared to act in any new direction which the situation may demand. As a rule they would be ordered to return to their original position in reserve as soon as their task is completed.

8. MINES.

Should the enemy fire a mine in or near our trenches, the side nearest our line of the crater thus formed will be immediately occupied by the nearest troops. This order will be made known to all ranks.

9. FIRING BY DAY AND NIGHT.

By day men will only fire when a target offers itself. If the enemy is in the habit of showing himself at any particular point the attention of the platoon commander should be drawn to it. The latter will inform the battalion sniping officer who will tell off a sniper's post to watch the spot.

By night all firing must be organised. If the enemy is believed to be working on his trenches or wire, the company commander will give directions to his platoon commanders to fire five rounds rapid at certain stated times. He will first ascertain that no patrols from neighbouring companies will be out at these hours.

A certain number of fixed rifles will be placed in every trench and fired by the sentries. These rifles will be laid on certain selected spots.

Indiscriminate firing by day or night is forbidden.

If the enemy attacks, rapid fire will be opened without waiting for orders.

10. COMPANY MEETINGS.

Officers commanding companies will hold meetings of their platoon commanders and N.C.Os. each evening in the trenches. Only a few officers and N.C.Os. should be present at each meeting. At these meetings the following points should be discussed:—

Work required to place our trenches in a better state of defence and to improve the comfort of the men.

Work to be done during the next 24 hours.

It is essential that all work which has to be carried out at night is explained to all N.C.Os. in daylight.

Any alteration noticed in the enemy's trenches or wire.

What steps can be taken to annoy and harass the enemy.

Action in case of attack.

11. WORK ON TRENCHES.
Work on trenches should as far as possible be carried out during daylight.

12. GARRISONS OF TRENCHES.
It is an invariable rule that, during daylight, the front line trenches should be held as lightly as is compatible with safety. At night the garrison must be strengthened.

The actual strength of garrisons will be governed by the tactical situation and by the number of support and communicating trenches at hand.

With proper support and communicating trenches only sentries and snipers should be in the front line trenches during daylight. To these will be added bombers if there are any old communicating trenches leading to the enemy's lines, or if the proximity of the enemy demands their presence.

13. DISCIPLINE.
(a) Sleeping in the front line trenches will not be allowed unless there is an absence of support trenches.

(b) No dug-outs will be constructed without the permission of the battalion commander. All dug-outs must be made splinter-proof. Work on them will not be commenced until sufficient material is at hand. If it can be avoided dug-outs will not be constructed in the fire trenches.

(c) No man will leave the trenches without permission from an officer. This order will be made known to all ranks.

(d) Cooking should not take place in the front line trenches. Whenever possible cooking will be done under company arrangements in order that the men may have their meals at regular hours.

Washing and shaving should be carried out in support trenches when possible.

(e) All parties moving within the trench area will be correctly marched by an officer or N.C.O.

(*f*) Orderly room should be held daily in the trenches unless circumstances render this impossible.

(*g*) Sentries are strictly forbidden to wear any covering over the ears.

(*h*) An officer will always be present when an issue of rum takes place.

(*i*) Equipment will never be taken off in the front line trenches. In support trenches equipment may be removed at the discretion of battalion commanders.

(*j*) Sentries will remain standing at all times unless the height of the parapet renders this impossible.

(*k*) All parties, with the exception of stretcher-bearers, moving in the trench area will wear their arms and equipment. Orderlies may be excused wearing their equipment at the discretion of commanding officers.

(*l*) The wearing of cotton bandoliers by working parties and orderlies is forbidden, nor are these bandoliers to be hung up in the trenches.

(*m*) Ammunition must be kept in a thoroughly clean state. If the ammunition is not clean jambs will occur. Ammunition will be frequently inspected.

(*n*) The "undercutting" of trenches is strictly forbidden. Drains will always be cut down the centre of a trench and not at the sides.

(*o*) When mining is in progress in any of the trenches occupied by the Brigade the sandbags filled with earth from the mine will on no account be used in the front trenches or other points which are visible to the enemy.

14. RECONNAISSANCE AND PATROLLING.

The best security against attack is active patrolling and constant observation of the enemy's lines, so that he cannot undertake any new work without steps being taken to prevent its continuance.

The enemy's wire will be constantly patrolled to ensure that he has cut no gaps in it with a view to launching an attack.

Patrols will also frequently visit our wire to ensure that it is efficient.

The front of our own fire parapet should be examined nightly.

Two of the platoons of a company are detailed each night to find one patrol, of one N.C.O. and three men each, for each half of the night. The patrol found by the left platoon always goes on patrol first, so that there may be no mistake who goes out first.

Two or more zig-zag paths are constructed through the wire, by which patrols must either go out or come in. This is in order to let the sentries know that anyone trying to enter somewhere else, along the trench, is an enemy and should be fired on. Patrols returning from patrol work halt outside the wire, and the commander then advances by himself up to the sentry post till challenged. When the sentry is satisfied as to his identity, he returns to his patrol and brings it in.

15. INFORMATION.

Every effort will be made by means of patrols, field-glasses, &c., to ascertain information about the enemy, his trenches and wire. Any alteration in the enemy's lines must be reported, and if any of the enemy are seen a report will be sent in stating what dress they were wearing. The importance of forwarding all such information will be impressed on all ranks.

16. SNIPING.

In every battalion a Sniping section will be formed, consisting of 1 officer and 64 N.C.Os. and men. The officer will carry out the duties of Intelligence officer to his battalion. He will render a daily report to his Commanding Officer containing the following information:—

Number of casualties known to have been inflicted on the enemy.
Number and location of snipers' posts.
Any alterations in the enemy's trenches or wire.
Number of telescope rifles in possession.
Number and location of fixed rifles and rifle batteries in action.
Any activity by the enemy.

Battalion Sniping Officers will get into close touch with Artillery Observing Officers within their sectors, and will give every assistance to them.

17. ARTILLERY SUPPORT.

As a general rule a forward observing officer of an 18-pounder battery will be quartered at or near Battalion H.Q.

Requests for retaliation should be made to this officer and Brigade H.Q. should be warned of the action taken.

Fire from howitzers and heavy batteries can, except in the case of the S.O.S. signal, only be obtained through Brigade H.Q. If retaliatory fire is required from howitzers it must be stated on what point it is wished that the fire should be directed.

Any trench mortaring by the enemy should be immediately reported to the officer commanding our trench mortars.

'Where did you get that hat ?',
from the Christmas 1915
edition of The Dump, trench
magazine of 23rd Division.
Both the French (left) and
British (right) armies adopted
steel helmets in 1915, British
issues being completed for troops
at the front in early 1916.

18. "S.O.S." & "TEST" SIGNALS.

In the event of an infantry attack by the enemy, a mine being fired, or other emergency, the S.O.S. signal will be sent by the quickest route to the Field Artillery Battery covering the trenches concerned.

The signal will be followed by the number of the trench, e.g., "S.O.S. B4."

The signal will be repeated to Battalion H.Q. who will transmit it to Brigade H.Q.

On receipt of the S.O.S. signal all batteries covering the trenches concerned will open a concentrated fire on the enemy's front line.

When necessity for fire no longer exists a message to this effect will be sent to the Artillery and to Brigade H.Q.

In order to test the efficient working of the artillery lines "Test" messages will frequently be sent from the trenches to the supporting battery.

The number of the trench will always be sent, e.g., "Test A 6."

The test will consist of one round of shrapnel fired on the "night line" of the battery. No target will be given by the officer in the trenches.

The time taken from the handing in of the message until the shell bursts will be carefully noted and reported to Battalion H.Q. The O.C. battalion will enter the results of all tests in his daily report. He will give the exact time at which the test was sent and will state whether it was a "direct" or an "indirect" test. A "direct" test is from trench to battery. An "indirect" test is from trench via Battalion H.Q. to battery.

19. VERMOREL SPRAYERS.

One man will be detailed to look after each sprayer. A spare tin of solution will be kept with each sprayer. Medical officers will periodically inspect both sprayers and solution.

Attacking round a traverse as the lead 'bayonet man' of a bombing party.

20. HOSTILE ARTILLERY FIRE.

In reporting activity by the enemy's artillery it is necessary to state:—

  (i) The time at which shelling began and when it ceased.
  (ii) Your own position.
  (iii) Whether howitzer or gun.
  (iv) Direction from which shells arrive. Compass bearing should be given if possible.
  (v) Whether shells burst in the air or on "graze."

In reporting results of our own fire, state:—

  (i) Your own position.
  (ii) Estimate distances short, over, right or left, in yards. Avoid vague statements.
  (iii) Whether gun or howitzer.
  (iv) Whether shrapnel or high explosive.

If shrapnel bursts in the air judge whether range is correct by the splash of the bullets on the ground and not by the burst.

21. AIRCRAFT.

On the approach of any of the enemy's aircraft three blasts will be blown on a whistle. This will be the signal for all ranks to keep perfectly still.

One blast on a whistle will indicate that the aircraft has moved away.

All aircraft belonging to the enemy will be heavily fired on by machine guns and rifles as long as they are within range, but no firing will take place without the order of an officer, who will first satisfy himself that the aircraft is hostile. Directions should be given to the men as to how many lengths in front of the aeroplane aim should be taken. If a "Zeppelin" is sighted a "priority" message will be sent to Brigade H.Q. reporting the fact, and stating approximately where the "Zeppelin" was seen and in what direction it was proceeding.

22. MAPS.

Maps with our own trenches marked on them will not be taken into the front line trenches.

23. TELEPHONE MESSAGES.

No messages regarding the action of our own artillery or other matters of an important nature will be sent by telephone to the fire trenches. Such messages will be sent by orderly. This is necessary because it has been found that the enemy has, at times, read our messages by induction.

The 'Pullman A1' was just one of many types of commercial trench armour that could be purchased by British officers. The practicality of such devices was often compromised by the weight of metal or other materials required to stop modern projectiles.

24. SIGNALLERS.

The Brigade Signalling Section is responsible for the maintenance of communication between Brigade H.Q. and battalions.

Brigade Signalling Officer is responsible for communications within the battalions.

All wires must be pinned in to the sides of trenches. Infantry wires on the S. and E. sides, and artillery wires on the N. and W. sides.

Pins for this purpose can be obtained from Brigade H.Q.

All wires will be labelled with the name of the battalion at least every fifty yards.

Officers in charge of battalion signallers are responsible that all disused or unlabelled wires within their areas are reeled up.

All wires will be patrolled at least once every 24 hours.

25. MEDICAL OFFICERS.

Medical Officers attached to battalions will, in addition to looking after the sick and wounded, be responsible for the sanitation of the trenches generally paying particular attention to the water supply and latrines. Battalion sanitary sections will work under the orders of the medical officer.

The medical officer will accompany the commanding officer periodically on his visits round the trenches.

Stretcher bearers are responsible that the rifles and equipment (including field glasses, wire cutters, &c.) of all men who are wounded are taken with them to the dressing station. The medical officer will instruct the N.C.O. i/c stretcher bearers to see that this order is carried out.

The arms and equipment of wounded men will be sent to the field ambulance with them, the ammunition having first been removed from pouches and magazines. Field glasses, wire cutters, &c., will not be sent to the field ambulance but will be sent to Battalion Headquarters.

The arms and equipment of men who are killed will be collected at Battalion H.Q. and handed over to the Quartermaster for return to the Base.

26. RATIONS.

Tinned rations for 24 hours are taken into the trenches by the relieving party.

The rations for the following day are brought up daily to a point in rear after dark, and are carried up into the trenches in sand bags by a special party detailed from the reserve or from the section on duty in each platoon.

It is a great convenience if the Quartermaster makes up each company's rations into sand bags for them. Also if the sand bags have the company marked with a piece of tin with another circular piece of tin underneath to denote the 1st, 2nd, 3rd or 4th platoon of the company; light is then not necessary when sorting the rations.—Example: No. 10 Platoon ration bag is marked C.

27. EMPTY CARTRIDGE CASES AND RUBBISH

At intervals throughout the trenches sand bags will be hung up as receptacles for empty cartridge cases and chargers. Others will be hung up for the collection of rubbish. Sand bags to be labelled accordingly. All empty cases and chargers thus collected will be sent each evening to Battalion H.Q. for transmission to the Base.

28. DRESS, &c.

Men must be properly dressed at all times and as smart and clean as circumstances will allow.

All men must shave daily.

Discipline as regards saluting, standing to attention, &c., will receive as much attention in the trenches as in billets.

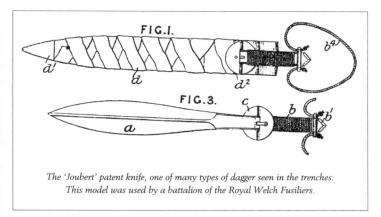

The 'Joubert' patent knife, one of many types of dagger seen in the trenches. This model was used by a battalion of the Royal Welch Fusiliers.

29. PRISONERS.

Should any prisoners be captured they will be immediately searched, and all documents found on them will be forwarded to Brigade H.Q. without delay. Germans usually carry all documents in the skirt pockets of their tunics. A telephone message will be despatched to Brigade H.Q. stating to what regiment the prisoners belong.

All ranks will be warned that, should they find themselves in the hands of the enemy, it is only necessary for them to give their number, name and regiment. No other information whatever will be given.

30. RETURNS.

The following returns are due at Brigade H.Q. daily when in the trenches:—

At 5.15 a.m.—	Situation and wind—	By
At 11.0 a.m.—	Strength and casualty return—	By
	Daily report on typed form—	By orderly
	Artillery intelligence report—	By orderly
At 4.0 p.m.—	Situation and wind—	By telephone
At 5.30 p.m.—	Intelligence report—	By orderly or telephone
At 9.0 p.m.—	Return of material required for trench construction to be sent up the following evening—	By telephone

Activity by the enemy's aeroplanes will always be reported.

31. MESSENGERS.

One man per platoon (or more if necessary) are detailed to carry messages along the firing trench. This is to prevent shouting. They wake up the sections off duty in case of alarm.

One man is told off per platoon to issue ammunition in case of attack.

32. WATER.

Water in the vicinity of trenches is generally contaminated and must be proscribed. Sentries should be placed to prevent its use. Drinking water should be stored in the trenches in rum jars and barrels. It can usually be brought up in the battalion water carts to a short distance from the trenches by night, if a good reliable supply is not available close at hand.

33. SANITATION.

Every effort must be made to maintain and improve the sanitary conditions of the trenches and their vicinity.

Latrines should be on the bucket system and be evacuated nightly. This should be sited as far back from the trenches as is consistent with safety. An orderly should be in charge and be responsible that they are kept sweet by disinfectants.

All refuse, empty tins, and rubbish, should be placed in properly appointed rubbish sacks or receptacles, and these should be removed at night time and their contents buried.

34. ISSUE OF RUM.

The issue of rum in the trenches is as a rule undesirable. It is difficult to supervise, and leads to drunkenness. If issued just before the men go on duty it makes them drowsy and unfit for the alert duties of a sentry. If it is considered necessary it is best issued in the morning, just after the men have been dismissed from standing to arms.

35. CARE OF FEET.

Officers Commanding Companies should carry out frequent inspections, and see that their subordinate commanders do the same. Every man should take a spare pair of socks to the trenches, and every opportunity should be taken to change the socks if the feet get wet. A good way to carry socks is to put one under the jacket on each shoulder. This prevents the equipment "cutting into the shoulders." If only the pair of socks being worn is available it will be found refreshing to occasionally stretch the socks and turn them inside out. It will also be found refreshing to soap the socks or to put Boric Powder in the boots.

E. B. NORTH

Major,

Brigade-Major,

124th INFANTRY BRIGADE.

CHAPTER 6

Notes on Minor Enterprises, March 1916
Issued by General Staff G.H.Q., March, 1916.

The following notes have been compiled as a result of the experience gained in certain minor operations carried out during the past few months.

No definite rules for the conduct of such operations can be laid down, but the suggestions contained in these notes may be useful as a guide in future enterprises.

General Principles.

1. Success in a minor operation against the enemy's trenches depends mainly on careful selection and reconnaissance of the objective and on a thorough working out of all the details of the operation beforehand.

The selection and reconnaissance of the objective, as well as the concealment of our intentions, can only be carried out successfully, if superiority in patrol work between the lines has been established.

The choice of an objective will depend on various considerations, *e.g.*:—

     (*a*) The existence of a covered approach to some portion of the enemy's line;

     (*b*) A lack of vigilance discovered by our patrols;

     (*c*) The isolation of some portion of the enemy's line, so that it cannot easily be supported or reinforced.

     (*d*) Facilities for supporting the operation by artillery, trench mortar, or machine gun fire.

The objective must be limited and definite, and all details regarding the action of the party, *e.g.*, what points are to be blocked, how side trenches are to be dealt with, must be worked out beforehand.

Ample time, at least a week, is required for preparation of the enterprise. Surprise is probably the most important factor in these attacks, and the utmost secrecy must be maintained regarding the preparations. Originality and imagination in planning and carrying out an enterprise should be allowed full scope, provided the principles underlying the plan are sound.

The number of men employed varies according to the nature and extent of the objective. The German trenches have been entered by patrols of from 2 to 8 men, and for the purpose of securing an identification or obtaining information on some definite point, *e.g.*, the existence of a suspected mine shaft, a small patrol may be sufficient. Raids on the enemy's trenches have been made by parties varying from 80 to 800 men, either with or without the co-operation of artillery.

Attacks by separate parties at different points are difficult to synchronise and are not recommended.

Artillery may be used:—

> (*a*) To cut the wire previous to the attack. In this case the wire should be cut at several other points besides the one to be attacked. The gaps cut should be kept open by machine gun or Lewis gun fire.
> (*b*) To form a barrage round the point of attack.

Gas and smoke may also be used to divert the enemy's artillery fire from the point of attack or to form a barrage on the flank of the attacking force.

It is seldom advisable to persevere in a minor enterprise if the enemy are found ready and prepared.

Preparations.

2. The preparation and working out of the details of a minor operation should be left as much as possible to the unit engaged upon the enterprise. But the Brigade or Divisional Staff must check the scheme when it has been prepared.

Officers and men selected to take part in the operation should, when possible, be volunteers. The men should be quartered together in a comfortable billet for the week preceding the operation.

All information referring to the front on which the operation is to take place must be carefully studied. This can be obtained from:—

> **Aeroplane photographs.**
> **Reports of patrols.**
> **Statements of prisoners.**
> **Trench log books.**
> **Reports of snipers and artillery observers.**

The selected objective must be kept under close observation and every endeavour made to ascertain the enemy's patrol beats, listening posts, grenade posts, machine gun positions, etc., the times when his reliefs take place, at what hours he is least on the alert, etc.

Weather forecasts should be studied and the almanac consulted. Very dark nights are unsuitable, as it is difficult for men to find their way or recognise each other.

Watches should be synchronised at intervals for several days before the attack and an hour or two before the assault is timed to take place.

If artillery, trench mortars or machine guns are to co-operate, they must register on the points they will fire on, but this must be done so as not to attract the attention of the enemy to the point of attack. If the same points (and other points besides that where the attack will take place) have been fired on several times previously without any attack taking place, the enemy may notice nothing unusual on the night of the attack.

Training.

3. The men who are to take part in a minor operation must be given confidence. They must be taught:—

> (*a*) To lie outside our own wire;
> (*b*) To stand or remain in any position in which they may be found when enemy flares go up;
> (*c*) To crawl forward, going gradually farther each night;
> (*d*) To lie up under the enemy's parapet.

The raiding party must be practised over an area furnished with wire and trenches and as like the objective as possible.

Practice advances should take place at the same hour in the same formations and under the same conditions as in the proposed raid.

Cutting wire must be practised and the time which this takes must be carefully noted.

The action to be taken if the enemy is found to be prepared and it becomes necessary to abandon the enterprise, must be known to all ranks and practised.

Every man, or if the party is too large, all officers and N.C.O.'s. should, if possible, take part in a reconnaissance of the actual ground to be crossed and the time taken in reaching the German wire should be noted. Care must be taken, however, not to put the enemy on his guard.

Men should be practiced in grenade throwing, dealing with dug-outs, meeting grenade attacks in trenches and the open, using the bayonet in narrow trenches, and should be given rifle and revolver practice on the range.

They should be taught the use of German phrases such as "hands up", "come out".

All ranks should be warned that the enemy may challenge in English or French and may give the order "retire."

All information collected should be accessible to all ranks and this should include details on the following points:—

> Description of the enemy's trenches.
> Reports of other minor operations.
> Notes on the enemy's hand grenades.
> How to use and dismount the enemy's machine guns.
> German soldier's pay-book and identity disc (the identity disc is usually hung round the neck and the pay-book sewn in the skirt of the coat).
> Where gas cylinders are likely to be found.
> Description of the enemy's gas cylinders.
> Description of the enemy's flammenwerfer equipment.
> Description of the enemy's unit supposed to be holding the trenches to be attacked.
> Instructions as to what a soldier is bound to divulge if captured, viz: rank and name only.

Dress, Arms and Equipment.

4. All identification marks, or badges on the clothing or uniform, and all identity discs should be removed to prevent the enemy obtaining any useful information. For the purpose of recognition some special distinguishing mark or badge should be worn by all ranks, but this should not be visible to the enemy when the men are crawling forward to the attack.

Men's faces and hands should be darkened. Khaki woollen caps or Balaclava helmets have been found a suitable head-dress. Woollen gloves to be worn while crawling forward and thrown away on reaching the enemy's parapet have been found useful.

Men should be armed according to the tasks they are to perform. Bayonet men should carry rifles and bayonets and 50 rounds of ammunition. Revolvers, knobkerries and daggers have been used. Men to carry revolvers must be carefully trained in their use.

Electric torches fixed to the rifle with black insulating tape have been found useful for men detailed to clear dug-outs. The insulating tape conceals the bright metal parts of the torch and prevents short circuiting.

The raiding party should be provided with the most powerful wire cutters available. Men for wire cutting should be provided with leather hedging gloves.

In addition to the grenadiers, every man should carry two grenades.

Allocation of Tasks.

5. In addition to the assaulting party or parties, who actually enter the enemy's trenches, it has often been found advisable to have a support part at some suitable point between our front line and the point of attack, to establish liaison with the assaulting party, provide support or cover the withdrawal, evacuate prisoners etc.

There may also be a reserve party, which remains in our front line trenches, to give support if required, cover the withdrawal and meet any counter attack, which the enemy may make.

Every man must be detailed for a definite task. Raiding parties may include the following:—

> Wire cutting parties.
> Parties to clear enemy's trench, composed of bayonet men and grenadiers.
> Parties to clear the enemy's dugouts.
> Blocking parties.
> Rifle grenade men.
> Lewis gun detachment.
> R.E. party for demolition purposes.
> Parties of scouts to watch the flanks.
> A telephone squad or messengers.
> Stretcher parties to bring in wounded.

Men may also be specially detailed for any of the following tasks:—

> To look for gas cylinders (carrying ropes to drag them back with if found).
> To look for mine shafts.
> To destroy machine guns.
> To take prisoners or secure identifications.
> To bring in "loot".
> To carry ladders or cut steps to provide an exit out of deep enemy trenches.
> To carry mats or ladders for crossing wire.
> To carry light bridges.
> To lay out white tape or chloride of lime to indicate return route.

Support of Attack.

6. Artillery preparation before the attack will usually be confined to wire cutting.

The scheme for the support of the attack by artillery barrages, or by trench mortars, machine guns, grenade throwers or rifle grenades, must be worked out in the greatest detail and must be known to all concerned. Very careful arrangements for timing are necessary. A definite time may be agreed on beforehand for the commencement of the artillery action, or fire may be opened according to a pre-arranged scheme on the order of the O. C. Assaulting Party or an infantry officer in our front line trenches, who is responsible for the arrangements for the attack.

Supporting fire may be directed:—

(a) On the flanks and rear of the area assaulted;

(b) On main communication trenches and roads by which the enemy might bring up reserves;

(c) On the actual points raided, after the attacking party has withdrawn, to cover the withdrawal and cause loss to the enemy who have collected for a counter attack.

Units on the flanks of the raiding force must be fully informed of the situation and may co-operate by keeping down any rifle or machine gun fire directed against the flanks of the attack.

Miscellaneous Points.

7. (a) Each raiding party should have a separate password and the name of the leader of the party should be known to all.

(b) The signal to retire from the enemy's trenches must be distinctive. A syren whistle has been found effective.

(c) The enemy should be kept under continued observation from dusk on the night of the operation until the attack is made, and the main party should not advance till scouts have ascertained that the way is clear. If the wire has to be cut by hand, it should be done by a special party, and the main party should not advance till the wire is reported cut.

(d) Every precaution should be taken on the night of the assault to maintain normal quietness in our lines and to ensure that no indication whatever is given to the enemy of anything unusual.

(e) Men with coughs and colds should be eliminated from a raiding party.

(f) The employment of dummies to deceive the enemy and draw fire to a flank has been found useful.

CHAPTER 7

Notes on the Tactical Employment of Machine Guns and Lewis Guns, March 1916

Issued by the General Staff at G.H.Q.

INTRODUCTION.

1. The experience of the present war has shown that the general principles as regards the employment of machine guns laid down in Infantry Training 158–163 are perfectly sound, and remain unaltered by the introduction of the machine gun company organization.

The notes issued in June, 1915 (C.D.S. 36), were compiled as a result of the experience of the early stages of the war to show how machine guns had been used during the period of open fighting and with what results.

In view of the increase in the numbers of machine guns with infantry units, it is most important that all commanders should understand thoroughly the main principles of their use. These are, therefore, briefly recapitulated in this pamphlet, with the addition of certain notes on the further experience gained in trench warfare, on indirect fire, and on the special characteristics of the Lewis gun.

A comprehensive Machine Gun Manual is in course of preparation in England.

GENERAL PRINCIPLES.

2. *Characteristics of Machine Guns.*—Their chief characteristics are—
    (*a*) Their fire power, which is their only method of employment.
    (*b*) The nature of such fire.
    (*c*) The small target they offer and the ease with which they can be concealed.

(a) *Method of Employment.*—Machine guns, acting solely by fire, can prepare an attack or repulse an offensive, but cannot actually gain ground. This role always rests with the infantry, the only arm which is capable of moving across all obstacles.

It can, therefore, be said that, whenever action by fire alone is sufficient, it will be advantageous to use machine guns rather than infantry, reserving the latter for the combined operations of movement and fire.

The use of machine guns, therefore, economises infantry and consequently allows a considerably larger portion to be retained as a reserve.

Owing to the small number of its personnel, a machine gun team cannot arrange for its own local protection. If sent on a detached mission, or acting on an extreme flank, a machine gun officer should apply to the nearest unit for an escort of a few rifles.

The machine gun, to a great extent, is a weapon of opportunity, and these opportunities will be very rare if a purely passive attitude is adopted. Machine gunners must be trained to use their guns very boldly, and, to enable them to do so, they must be thoroughly instructed in the use of ground, concealment and selection of positions.

It is not intended to advocate the running of useless risks, nor should any precaution as to concealment be neglected.

(b) *Fire*.—Machine gun fire produces a dense, deep, but narrow cone of fire. By increasing the traverse, the cone becomes wider, but, owing to loss of density, the effect is reduced.

Machine gun fire will therefore have its maximum power against objectives which are narrow-fronted but deep. As infantry fights normally in thin lines, the above-named conditions can only be brought about by enfilade fire. Machine guns should endeavour to fire in a direction parallel to the probable front of the enemy, *i.e.*, from a flank.

As a general rule, frontal fires will only be directed against points which the enemy is obliged to pass, such as bridges, roads, defiles, approaches, communication trenches, &c.; that is to say, at points where the enemy is obliged to adopt a deep and narrow formation, or else when he is massed.

Only in exceptional circumstances should machine guns open fire at long ranges; normally they will withhold their fire in order to obtain surprise effect. At ranges up to 800 yards well directed machine gun fire is annihilating in its effect. A very high standard of fire discipline and fire control is necessary to obtain good effect at longer ranges.

Although the principle that machine guns should not open fire unless a good target presents itself still holds good, this must not be carried to extremes, or opportunities of inflicting both moral and material damage to the enemy may be lost. The tactical situation will guide the machine gun officer in his decision to open fire.

For instance, in a rearguard action he would engage a target which, in a defensive position, strongly held, would not justify his disclosing his position by opening fire.

Again, small parties of the enemy dribbling across open spaces to concentrate for an attack, or an extended line of infantry, may be fired on if their manœuvre is considered sufficiently threatening, although they present a bad target for machine gun fire.

It must be remembered that it is often impossible to see anything of the enemy; therefore positions which are likely to be occupied by him should be looked for and, if necessary, searched by the fire of well-concealed guns.

It is, of course, not only justifiable, but essential, that fire should be opened to assist the advance of our own infantry.

(c) *Concealment.*—On account of the small number of their personnel, machine gun sections can take advantage of very slight cover, and are consequently able to escape detection. Machine guns—much more so than infantry—possess the power of surprise, and can thus obtain greater effects.

Opening fire by surprise will be the rule, and machine guns must therefore avoid disclosing their positions by opening fire without good reason.

Flanking fire and surprise are the two conditions which must be sought for and obtained whenever possible.

(a) *During movement:*—

When on the move, machine gunners should try to disguise their identity as such by adopting the formation of the neighbouring troops. This, and any other means of escaping detection, should be constantly practised.

(b) *When in position:*—

(i) As few men as possible should be near the gun. It will usually be found that two men are quite sufficient.

(ii) When time, implements, &c., are available, guns should be dug in, but, unless it is possible to construct a really satisfactory emplacement, it is better to seek cover from view. A hastily made emplacement will merely serve to draw the attention of the enemy.

(iii) Masks and gloves will often facilitate concealment, especially when facing strong sunlight.

Every effort must be made to prevent machine guns being located by artillery. If, however, machine guns are shelled, their action will largely depend on the tactical situation. They may make a change in position of about 50 yards or they may temporarily cease fire, the guns and teams getting under cover; the latter will often deceive the enemy into thinking that they have been knocked out and enable them to get a good target later. A careful distribution of the gun numbers will minimise casualties.

When machine guns are moving, they should watch and avoid areas that are being swept by shell fire.

Machine guns which have been able to approach unseen to within close range of hostile artillery have caused them serious damage, because the gun shields have been penetrated by the bullets. Normally enfilade fire gives the best results against artillery. There are many instances of its successful employment, even at distant ranges.

3. *Co-operation.*—Co-operation is an essential feature in machine gun

tactics, both between the machine guns and other arms and between the guns themselves.

Grouping machine guns into companies, by centralizing control, facilitates the execution of a comprehensive scheme of machine gun co-operation in accordance with the needs of the tactical situation. The machine gun company commander must be thoroughly conversant with the situation. He should take every step to ensure co-operation, not only between the guns of his company, but between his company and machine guns on the flanks.

EMPLOYMENT OF MACHINE GUNS IN OPEN FIGHTING.

4. It must be borne in mind that trench warfare is only a phase of operations, and to arrive at a definite decision the enemy's forces must be driven from their trenches and crushed in the open. It is, therefore, of the utmost importance that men should be thoroughly trained in the handling of machine guns in the open.

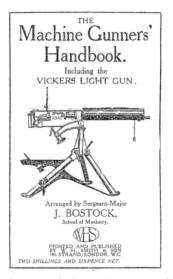

Advertisement for Sergeant Major J. Bostock's
Machine Gunner's Handbook, c.1914.
*Bostock was later promoted to Captain and
also produced other manuals.*

5. *With advanced guard.*—The duties of an advanced guard make it necessary that great fire power should be available when required. A large proportion of machine guns should therefore be allotted to advanced guards.

These machine guns should move well forward in the column, so that they may be able to get quickly into action.

The principal duties of machine guns with the advanced guard are to:—

> (*a*) Assist in driving back enemy forces by rapid production of great fire power at any required point;
>
> (*b*) Assist in holding any position gained until the arrival of the infantry;
>
> (*c*) Cover the deployment of the main body by holding the enemy on a wide front.

Lewis guns should be employed with the van-guard, the machine guns being with the main guard.

6. *In the attack.*—In order to obtain the best results from the machine guns, the machine gun company commander must be thoroughly acquainted with the plan of operations and must make a careful reconnaissance of the ground.

By use of maps and study of the ground through a telescope from positions in rear or on the flanks, he should endeavour to make himself familiar with the nature of the ground, the correct use of which may prove of decisive value.

Having made his reconnaissance, and having received instructions from the brigade commander, the brigade machine gun company commander will give definite orders to his section officers.

During the action he will keep in closest touch with the brigade commander.

In a battle of manœuvre, it will usually be found impossible to rely on telephones, and communication will usually be maintained by:—

Visual signalling.
Orderlies.

7. *Distribution of guns in the attack.*—The machine gun company commander may divide the guns under his command into groups:—

> (a) *Some to go forward with attacking infantry.*—i. The *number* of these will be governed by two factors, viz., the length of front and the nature of the ground.
>
> ii. The *time* of their advance will be determined by the nature of the ground and progress of the infantry.
>
> > These guns will be placed under the infantry battalion commanders concerned.
> >
> > It will usually be found inadvisable to move forward machine guns with the first line of infantry, and therefore the progress of the infantry must be carefully watched so as to bring forward the guns at the earliest possible moment.

In exceptional cases, when the ground is favourable, these guns may be able to push forward with the scouts and, by sudden bursts of fire, to assist the advance of the infantry.

iii. The role of these guns will be to:—

(*a*) Assist the infantry in obtaining superiority of fire.

(*b*) Make good the positions won.

(*c*) Pursue the enemy with fire.

(*d*) Cover re-organization of the infantry.

(*e*) Repel counter-attack.

(*f*) Cover retirement in the event of the attack proving unsuccessful.

iv. During the action, the section commander will keep in close touch with the commander of the unit to which he is attached.

(b) *Some to cover the advance of the infantry.*—These guns will provide covering fire for the infantry up to the last possible moment in the following ways:—

(*a*) By fire from the flanks.

(*b*) By overhead fire.

(*c*) By long range searching fire.

Great care must be exercised in (*b*) and (*c*) in order to avoid endangering our own troops.

Orders to the machine guns detailed for this task should always include general instructions to govern their action, after the task has been completed, pending receipt of further orders from the machine gun company commander.

(c) *Some may be kept as a reserve in the hands of the brigade commander.*—Owing to their characteristics, machine guns are most valuable as a reserve of fire power, and these guns may prove of the utmost value at the critical moment.

It must be remembered, however, that a great development of fire power is most useful in the opening stages of an attack, to cover the advance of the infantry, and it is a mistake to keep guns in reserve if they can be usefully employed in supporting the advance.

They may be used for long range searching fire on ground behind the enemy's line, which is likely to hold supports or reserves, but must be available to move forward at once, when required.

The great fire power of machine guns relative to the space they occupy, the rapidity with which they may be brought into or out of action and the ease with which they can change the direction of their fire render them especially suitable for the protection of threatened flanks and for filling gaps which may appear laterally or in depth. Any of the guns mentioned in the previous paragraph may at times be employed in this manner.

During an attack it may be advisable to continue to hold certain tactical points, which have been captured, until the attacking troops have made good their next objective. The characteristics of machine guns fit them for this duty; their use will avoid diminishing the strength and élan of the attacking infantry.

8. The machine guns that go forward with the attacking infantry will be under the control of the infantry commander to whom they are attached.

The remaining guns will be under the control of the machine gun company commander who acts under instructions from the Brigade Commander.

Machine gun officers must be acquainted with this principle in order to avoid dual control and consequent misunderstanding.

9. *Limbers and ammunition reserve.*—An officer should be in charge of the limbered wagons which carry the guns and the ammunition.

He should keep thoroughly in touch with the progress of the infantry so that he may be able to keep the wagons as close up as possible.

10. *Rear guard.*—As a rear guard will usually be required to hold positions with the minimum of men, a large proportion of machine guns should be allotted to them.

Experience has shown that well placed machine guns, supported by a few infantry only, will frequently hold up an advance for long periods.

In occupying a rear guard position with machine guns, the ordinary principles of defence apply, but the following points should be specially noted:—

(*a*) Wide field of fire.

(*b*) Machine guns concealed in the least obvious places.

(*c*) Covered lines of retirement must be reconnoitred.

(*d*) Limbered wagons should be close up to facilitate a hasty retirement.

(*e*) Positions in rear chosen before the machine guns retire from their forward positions.

(*f*) A proportion of the machine guns should occupy the positions in rear, before all the machine guns retire from forward position. (Thus the retirement of the last gun can be covered.)

(*g*) Pack transport is very useful.

11. *Village fighting.*—As soon as the infantry have made good one edge of a village, machine guns should be brought up in close support. They should then search windows, doorways, roofs, &c., likely to be held by the enemy.

Machine guns should be used to command cross-streets, &c., so as to guard against attack on the flanks or rear of the infantry. They should also be posted on the edges of the villages to prevent flank attacks, and when possible should be pushed forward well on the flanks, so as to command the exits from the village.

During village fighting use may be made of windows, doors, &c., as machine gun positions.

12. *Machine guns in the defence.*—When it has been decided to consolidate a position for defence a reconnaissance should be carried out. Some machine guns should be arranged as soon as possible in accordance with the nature of the ground, to form a complete belt of flanking machine gun fire along the front of the position. Also important concealed approaches and folds in the ground should be covered by machine guns.

Co-operation must be arranged with the Lewis guns of battalions, which can cover the less important approaches or small depressions or hollows which the machine guns cannot sweep.

Some machine guns should be kept in reserve. When the ground is suitable, these may be used for long range searching fire if the results are likely to justify the expenditure of ammunition, and the readiness of the guns to take up other tasks is not impaired. It will often be found advisable to prepare machine gun emplacements at important tactical points in rear of the front line and to detail guns for their occupation, if necessary. Preparation in this respect will facilitate a rapid readjustment of the line at any point.

Secondary positions and lines of retirement must be reconnoitred; steps must be taken to ensure that the teams are familiar with them. In case of a withdrawal becoming necessary, machine guns in supporting positions will cover the retirement of the infantry and guns in the front line. When the latter have occupied their secondary positions, they, in their turn, will cover the movement of the guns originally in support.

Communication must carefully be arranged throughout machine gun sections. Machine gun officers must keep in touch with battalion commanders and the machine gun company commander.

The following points should also be noted:—

1. **The position of the limbered wagon should be fixed and arrangements made for ammunition supply.**
2. **Range cards should be made for each gun.**
3. **The night and day gun positions will probably be different; the change from the one to the other should be made just after dark and just before dawn.**
4. **Arrangements for firing at night should be made.**
The variations that arise during the protracted defence of a position are dealt with under Trench Warfare.

13. *Occupation of various positions.*—Machine guns may be hidden in almost any position, but it is advisable to avoid places which are either obvious or easy to recognise, such as cross-roads or single objects. It is important that guns should merge into the surroundings and that straight edges or distinct shadows are not made.

Banks of rivers, canals and railways, ditches, folds in the ground, hedges, palings or walls, also mounds of earth may be used either to afford a covered line of approach and supply to a gun position or else a gun position itself. When firing over the top of the cover, greater protection is given if hollows are scooped out for the front tripod legs.

Houses may be employed in the following ways:—

> The gun may be placed in rear, firing through or round the sides of the house. When firing from a window, door or hole in the roof, the gun should be placed well back for concealment. A damp piece of cloth hung in front of the gun helps to conceal the flash. When firing from a cellar, care should be taken not to fire low, as this would cause a cloud of dust to rise and give away the position. A means of retirement and alternative emplacements should be arranged. Overhead fire and observation may often be obtained from high buildings.

Woods and crops provide cover from view, facilities for communication, and good lines of approach or supply. In neither case should guns be placed too near to the front edge. In woods it will often be possible to construct hasty overhead cover.

If a barricade has been constructed across a road, machine guns should not be put on the barricade itself but, if possible, in a concealed position to a flank from which they can enfilade the road.

Haystacks do not as a rule afford a very satisfactory position, but guns may be placed in a hollow in front, or behind, firing round the side, or else in a hollow on top, firing through the front face of the stack. A machine gun concealed in a field, which is covered with cornstalks, manure heaps, or mounds of roots is very hard to locate.

Wood stacks, planks, logs of trees, and farm implements may be used to conceal guns; cover from fire can often be obtained by the addition of bricks or sand bags.

Trees generally provide better observation posts than machine gun positions.

MACHINE GUNS IN TRENCH WARFARE.

In the defence.

14. *Co-operation* is essential to obtain the full value of a number of machine guns in the defence of a system of trenches. This will be facilitated by all the guns of the brigade company being placed in position by one officer, the commander of the company, in accordance with the scheme of defence arranged by the brigade commander. Co-operation between the flank guns of adjacent brigades will be arranged by consultation between the machine gun company commanders of the two brigades. Co-operation between the guns of

the brigade company and the Lewis guns of battalions will be arranged by consultation between the brigade machine gun company commander and battalion commanders.

The machine guns allotted for the defence of a battalion sector are placed under the command of the battalion commander, but the arrangement of the guns should not be altered without reference to the brigade commander. All company commanders and company officers must receive clear instructions on the scheme of machine gun defence in their sector, so that guns will not be used for purposes for which they are not intended.

Machine gun commanders must be informed when a bombardment by the artillery is to take place, so that they may be prepared to take advantage of any targets presented as a result of the bombardment.

15. *Distribution of guns.*—The extra fire power now placed in the hands of brigade and battalion commanders by the increase in the number of machine guns enables men to be economized in the front trenches, and a larger force thus left available for counter-attack.

A natural tendency is to place every available machine gun in the front-line trenches in order to establish an impassable curtain of fire in front of them. In the case of a bombardment, these trenches are liable to be very badly damaged and most of the machine guns may be destroyed. Any which have been located will certainly be put out of action. The tendency therefore to place an undue proportion of machine guns in the front line must be guarded against.

A proportion of machine guns must be placed in such a way that if, after a bombardment or by the use of asphyxiating gas, the enemy succeeds in penetrating our lines, his infantry, at every step of their advance, will be met with fire from machine guns which have been previously echeloned in depth, and will thus be compelled to stop.

It is not so necessary to cover a large area with fire, as to arrange for flanking fire from well-selected positions; this fire will sweep away the waves of hostile infantry as they try to push forward.

Commanders must therefore divide their machine guns between the front line and the ground in rear of it, and in each particular case must see that the emplacements blend with the surrounding ground and fit in with the general scheme of defence.

A proportion of the guns will be in reserve and allotted to defences in rear of the front system. They must be given a definite position and rôle in the defence scheme in case of attack. Where the ground admits, machine guns situated behind our front system of trenches may be able to render assistance by bringing fire on to hostile infantry as soon as they commence their advance. By this means the power of resistance of our front system can be supplemented by the fire of machine guns situated behind the zone of intense hostile bombardment.

Every advantage must be taken of periods in reserve to overhaul equipment and to carry on physical and mechanical training.

Guns in reserve may be used for indirect fire. Guns which form part of the defence of the front system should not be used for indirect fire.

17. [sic] Machine guns in trenches may be placed—

> (*a*) In the sides of a salient.
> (*b*) " " " re entrant.
> (*c*) At a bend in the trench.
> (*d*) In front of the trench.
> (*e*) In or near a support or communication trench.
> (*f*) In a straight line of trench firing through an oblique loophole.

Emplacements should be carefully concealed and made to harmonize with the surrounding works. A battle emplacement should be reserved for repelling an enemy attack, and should not be used for any other purpose.

Several alternative emplacements should be made, and should be marked "M.G." Emplacements must always be kept in good repair. Arrangements should be made to protect emplacements against grenade attacks.

16. *Taking over trenches.*—The machine gun company commander should reconnoitre the whole line, if possible, the day before taking over.

He should note the position of each machine gun, the area covered by its fire, all emplacements, dug-outs, ammunition depots, methods of communication, &c.

He will, subject to the brigadier's approval, issue his instructions to his section officers.

Machine gun companies should, when possible, be relieved at a different time to the infantry.

17. *Communication.*—The machine gun company commander must be in close touch with the sector commander and the section officers.

It is inadvisable to rely on the telephone system, which is usually broken during a bombardment, and all other forms of communication must be arranged, such as orderlies, visual signalling, &c.

As, however, any system is liable to break down, it is essential that all officers and gun commanders thoroughly understand the plan of action, so that they will be able to act on their own initiative.

18. During bombardments machine guns should be kept wrapped up in some waterproof cover in a dug-out. If no dug-out is available, guns should be placed in the bottom of the trench. The tripod may be left mounted in the battle emplacement.

The gun team should be distributed in order to prevent all being disabled by one shell.

Two men only are required to mount and work the gun.

19. The machine gun company commander will issue orders for the reliefs

within his company; as a rule these should not be carried out on the same night as the infantry reliefs. Machine gunners will probably require assistance in changing their gun equipment, for usually it is not satisfactory to change the teams alone.

Owing to the difficulty of obtaining trained machine gunners, it has been found advisable to have only three gunners at a time with each gun in the front line. It may be necessary to give them assistance in sentry work. The remaining three men should be kept in the central depot with the reserve ammunition until they are required. These two parties should relieve each other as often as necessary.

20. *Ammunition supply.*—The supply must be carefully thought out and arranged on the following lines. With each machine gun there should be eight full belts, and 4,000 rounds in unopened boxes ready to refill the belts; the remaining full belts, the belt-filling machine, and 4,000 rounds in unopened boxes should be with the reserve gunners at a central depot battalion headquarters or some other suitable place.

The above must be considered merely as a guide. The belt boxes with the gun should be distributed between the emplacement, the dug-out, and ammunition recesses; they should be protected from shell fire and the weather.

21. An order board should be placed in each emplacement. These can be obtained from Publication Section, Stationery Services, the number being S.S/102.

The following minor points require attention.

1. Every man should know the position of guns, depots and officers.
2. To avoid detection, portions of the gun which have worn bright should be painted or covered, and periscopes should not be used in the immediate vicinity of a battle emplacement.
3. Machine guns may be fired with fair accuracy resting on the parapet, but the gunners require practice to avoid faults in feed and ejection.
4. Tap traversing is often more efficient if it is irregular; the swing traverse should not be used at distances of over 300 yards.
5. Telescopes facilitate the detection of enemy machine guns. If one which is not causing serious damage is located, it should not be knocked out until an attack is intended. Its position should be reported to the artillery.
6. If overhead fire is used the garrison of the forward trenches should be warned.
7. Very pistols are invaluable for showing up night attacks.

22. *Emplacements.*—The type of emplacement to be erected in any site must be determined by the tactical situation, and the purposes for which the emplacement is to be used.

Open machine gun emplacements should be roughly 4 feet square. If the tripod legs are dug into the parapet the dimensions may be reduced. The platform must be from 1 foot 6 inches to 2 feet below the height over which the gun is to fire, according to the splay of the legs.

For emplacements with overhead cover, the following are absolute minimum dimensions:—

> 5 feet long to enable No. 1 to sit or stand comfortably behind the machine gun.
>
> 4 feet wide allows only just sufficient space for No. 2 to feed the machine gun.

The minimum clearance between the bottom of the loophole and the overhead cover, which will allow the raising of the cover of the gun, to remedy stoppages during firing is, for the Maxim, 2 feet. All emplacements should be made with this amount of clearance, as although a smaller clearance is sufficient for the Vickers, it is necessary that the emplacements should be suited for either gun.

The loophole must not be less than 9 inches in height to allow the firer to take a sight on to the target. Other dimensions of the loophole depend on the degree of traverse required and the thickness of the parapet.

The most important factor that governs the construction of machine gun emplacements is the question of *concealment*. The emplacement must look like the remainder of the parapet, and must not project above it. In some places, however, they may be made to simulate certain natural objects, such as mounds of earth or heaps of straw.

Aeroplane photographs should be studied to see if the emplacements are noticeable.

Loopholes may be made to harmonize with their surroundings, by means of carefully painted wire gauze, close mesh rabbit wire, a hinged or push-over trap door. Each of these should be set at the same angle as the rest of the parapet; the two latter should have interlaced in or attached to them grass, torn sandbag, or whatever else may lie in the vicinity. In all cases straight edges should be avoided. Loopholes can also be concealed by being blocked up with sandbags full of straw, or by being defiladed.

When the parapet consists entirely of earth it should be 6½ feet thick. If, in order to obtain a relatively large traverse without unduly increasing the size of the loophole, the emplacement is placed further forward into the parapet, the latter must be strengthened by bags full of broken brick, or by steel plates.

Head cover to be efficient should not be less than 1 foot in height.

23. *Dug-outs.*—Machine gun dug-outs should be 6 feet by 4 feet by 4 feet high. There should, if possible, be two to each gun position.

Recesses for the machine gun, spare parts, and a proportion of belt boxes, should be provided in the dug-out itself.

Ammunition recesses should be provided at the emplacement, and at other points in the vicinity, to give sufficient distribution. Those exposed to the weather may be rendered waterproof by roof felting or biscuit tins.

In the absence of a dug-out, a wooden recess for the gun may be provided in the trench, or in a shell slit.

Some notes on the construction of dug-outs and machine gun emplacements will be found in "Notes on Trench Warfare for Infantry Officers."

In the Attack.

24. The machine gun company commander must make a careful reconnaissance of the ground and study the enemy's trench system by the aid of trench maps and aeroplane photographs. Special attention must be paid to the position of enemy machine guns, known or suspected. The machine gun company commander should be able to judge the likely places for hostile machine guns to be located. He must also decide what special emplacements or works will be required for our own machine guns according to the plan of attack. These must be taken in hand as soon as the general plan has been decided.

Clear and definite orders must be issued to all machine guns as to their role and these should also be known to all taking part in the attack.

25. The rôle of machine guns in attack is to:—

    I. Assist the artillery, where possible.

    II. Provide covering fire for attacking infantry, and keep down flanking fire.

    III. Fill up gaps which may occur laterally or in depth.

    IV. Assist in consolidation of position won and repel counter attacks.

It is most important that all machine guns are allotted a definite task and given definite orders.

The guns of the brigade company may be allotted as follows:—

    I. Some to cover the advance by firing on enemy's parapet from the flanks, an advanced position, or commanding positions in rear, and to engage enemy machine guns on flanks.

        These guns should cover retirement if assault fails.

    II. Some to follow up assaulting infantry.

        Lewis guns only will go forward at first with the infantry, but some of the machine guns should be ready to go forward immediately, when the hand to hand fighting is finished. These guns should not open fire before the advance, and the line of advance should be carefully selected beforehand. They may also be employed to fill gaps and consolidate tactical points in rear of assaulting troops.

III. Some guns may be held in reserve at the commencement under the brigade commander, and may be used for firing from positions in rear, on points where enemy are likely to mass for counter attack. Guns should never, however, be kept in reserve, if they can be usefully employed in assisting the advance from the outset.

The officer in charge of guns in reserve must keep in close touch with brigade headquarters and be ready to go forward at once, when required.

During the preliminary bombardment the machine guns can render considerable assistance by preventing the repair of wire entanglements and damaged parapets, by direct or indirect fire. It may also be found possible to interfere with enemy reliefs or reinforcements, by bringing indirect fire to bear on communication trenches, and roads used by the enemy.

Depots for spare gunners, ammunition, minor repairs, and belt-filling machine should be arranged in good dug-outs. Each depot should be under a N.C.O., and the whole under an officer, who will push forward depots as required.

NOTES ON THE TACTICAL HANDLING OF LEWIS GUNS.

26. *Characteristics of machine guns and automatic rifles.*—The characteristics of a weapon determine its tactical handling, and in order to arrive at the best methods of using machine guns and automatic rifles respectively, it is necessary to compare their characteristics.

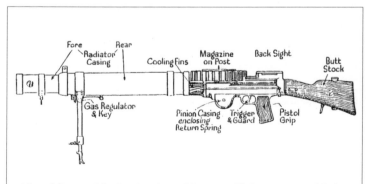

Manual diagram of the American-designed Lewis gun. The Lewis was one of the first 'light' machine guns: its increasing use was one of the factors which allowed the development of more flexible tactics.

The principal characteristic of the machine gun is its ability to produce *rapid and sustained fire*. Provided water and ammunition are available, a machine gun is capable of keeping up a rapid fire for a very considerable period.

On the other hand, an automatic rifle (of which the Lewis gun is a type), though capable of extremely rapid fire, is incapable of sustaining this fire for long. This necessitates, therefore, the use of short bursts of fire as the normal practice.

Its inability to sustain fire is primarily due to the fact that a water jacket is not provided (in order to economise weight) and the gun consequently becomes hot very quickly. Further, owing to their lightness, the working parts will not stand constant vibration to the same extent as those of the machine gun.

A further difference between the two weapons is in the type of mounting supplied. To increase its mobility the Lewis gun is provided with a light tripod, whereas the machine gun has the heavier Mark IV tripod.

The fixed platform provided by the use of this latter tripod enables the machine gun to be used for overhead fire, a form of fire for which the Lewis gun is unsuitable.

27. *Methods of employment.*—The differences in characteristics outlined above suggest the best uses to which the Lewis gun can be put. *It must be clearly understood that the Lewis gun cannot take the place of the machine gun.* It is a supplement to, and not a substitute for the machine gun.

It is necessary, in considering the uses of this weapon, to regard it from two points of view, *i.e.*, in trench warfare and open fighting.

The former will be dealt with first, not because it is the most important, but because it is the form of warfare in which we are now engaged.

28. *In trench warfare.*—Lewis guns should be used in a defensive line to economise infantry and to supplement the machine guns of the brigade company, not to take their place. They can be used in co-operation with the guns of the brigade company to sweep depressions, covered approaches, &c., on which these guns cannot fire. Lewis guns fire over the parapet and can therefore often sweep ground invisible from a machine gun emplacement, which is usually sited near ground level and therefore has a low command. There must be the closest co-operation between the battalions and the commander of the brigade machine gun company over the choice of the positions and tasks for Lewis guns.

As Lewis guns are company weapons, their number in the front line will be determined by the number of companies holding it.

Owing to the mobility of the Lewis gun, and the absence of a fixed platform, emplacements, in the ordinary acceptation of the term, are not required. The Lewis gun can be fired off its light mounting over any portion of the parapet with very little preliminary preparation and its fire can be brought to bear on an object very rapidly; a much greater liberty of action can therefore be allowed to this weapon than to the machine gun.

Although emplacements are unnecessary, definite "firing places" must be prepared, either by means of loopholes or in depressions in the parapet, defiladed from the front if possible.

In allocating Lewis guns to a portion of the defence, certain fronts should be given to them, and the teams should be thoroughly familiar with their "firing places," and the ground to be swept from each.

It is just as essential to keep Lewis guns under cover during a bombardment as it is to keep machine guns and their teams. In the case of the former weapon, however, as there are no definite emplacements, greater choice is possible in the selection of the spot for the shelters, provided the guns can come into action without delay.

The object of strong points is to bring a sudden and intense fire on the enemy from an unexpected direction if he has succeeded in breaking through the front line of defence. Machine guns are more suitable than Lewis guns for this purpose, owing to their greater capacity for sustained fire. Lewis guns can, however, be used in places affording only slight cover, and will also provide a mobile reserve of fire for use as required.

29. *In the attack.*—(a) *The attack from trenches.*—Owing to its lightness and the small target it offers, the Lewis gun is of great value in an attack. It is particularly adapted for providing covering fire from the front during the first stage of an attack. Lewis gunners, under cover of darkness, smoke, or artillery bombardment, may be able to creep out in front and establish themselves in shell holes, ditches, crops, long grass, &c., where it will be difficult for them to be detected, and where they will be able to fire on enemy machine gun emplacements, loopholes and parapets generally, and so assist the infantry to advance. Covering fire on the flanks of the attack must, however, be provided by machine guns as they can keep up a sustained fire from stationary platforms on previously considered objectives.

It is inadvisable to send forward any machine guns or Lewis guns with the first line of attacking infantry, but as soon as the infantry have got into the enemy's trenches, Lewis guns should be pushed up as rapidly as possible; they can provide the necessary fire while the infantry is re-organising and preparing the enemy's captured trench and will be especially useful on the flanks. They will, in fact, as far as their nature allows, take the place of machine guns, till the latter arrive to consolidate the position won.

Special instructions should be given to Lewis gunners to look for enemy machine guns and concentrate their fire upon them.

Lewis guns will also be of great value in minor operations from trenches and in supporting grenade attacks.

(b) *The attack in open warfare.*—In open fighting both sides will strive to obtain superiority of fire as early as possible; the addition of mobile fire power to the infantry by the possession of Lewis guns will materially assist them in their task.

Although in trench warfare it will usually be inadvisable to send forward Lewis guns with the leading line, owing to the short distance to be traversed and to the fact that there are obstacles such as barbed wire to be passed, in open warfare, where attacks will probably be made over long distances, and where the enemy's position is only hastily entrenched, it will be possible to push forward Lewis guns with the leading line, *the gunners moving and appearing to the enemy as ordinary riflemen.* Lewis guns pushed forward in this way will be able to provide covering fire for the infantry and will thus help them to advance.

Where ground is suitable, it may sometimes be possible for Lewis gunners to precede the attacking infantry, and opportunities to carry this out should be carefully looked for.

An opportunity for pushing forward Lewis guns may occur when an advance is held up or a hostile counter attack develops. In this way superiority of fire may often be obtained without incurring the loss incidental to sending up strong reinforcements to the front line.

30. *Summary.*—To summarise, Lewis guns will be of great value for the following purposes:—

- (i) To supplement the fire of infantry and machine guns.
- (ii) To economise infantry in trench warfare and in defensive positions.
- (iii) Firing from the parapet to command ground which cannot be swept by machine gun fire.
- (iv) To provide covering fire from the front during an attack.
- (v) To assist in the consolidation of positions won, and to cover the re-organisation of the attacking troops.
- (vi) For small enterprises, where the weight and visibility of the machine gun would render the latter unsuitable.
- (vii) As a means of reinforcing a line of infantry with additional fire power, under circumstances where the deployment and sending forward of more men would result in heavy losses.
- (viii) To provide a mobile "reserve of fire" in the hands of company commanders.

It should never be forgotten that the Lewis gun like the machine gun is a weapon of opportunity, and that surprise is the chief element of success in its use.

CHAPTER 8

Games
for Use with Physical Training Tables
and Training in Bombing, 1916

Issued with Army Orders dated 1st October 1916.

GENERAL REMARKS.

The essence of the following games is that they should be conducted with the utmost amount of energy and the rigid observance of all the details connected with them.

Executed in this way, they inculcate discipline and develop quickness of brain and movement, whereas, if carelessly carried out, they may do more harm than good.

A game may be introduced into the daily P.T. Table to prevent monotony, either before or after the Marching and Jumping Exercises or in place of them, according to the time available.

Games should not be continued for too long, and must not be carried out to the detriment of P.T. proper. Maximum time devoted to games during a Table should never exceed 10 minutes.

1. JUMPING THE BAG.

Formation.—The players stand in a circle at close intervals and facing inward.

Apparatus.—A light rope 5 to 8 yards long, to one end of which is attached a small bag of canvas or leather filled with sand and weighing about 1 lb.

Method of Playing.—The Instructor stands in the centre of the ring and swings the bag round, gradually paying out the rope until it becomes necessary for the players to jump to avoid it. The direction in which the bag is swung should be varied. The rate of swinging as well as height of the bag from the ground should be gradually increased. The object of the players is, of course, to avoid being caught by the rope or bag and brought to the ground.

Common Faults.

Some of the players stand outside the ring, the bag thus not passing under their feet.

2. SIMPLE RELAY RACE.

(a) **Formation.**—Two parallel lines are marked out about 20 to 50 yards apart.

Each team is divided into two parts containing an equal number of players. These are drawn up on the parallel lines, facing one another and extended at intervals of about 1 yard.

Method of Playing.—On the word "Go," the left hand man of each team drawn up on the one line, races to and touches the outstretched hand of the man immediately opposite him. As soon as his hand has been touched, the latter races similarly to the next man opposite, and so on, the team whose last man first crosses the line being the winners.

(b) **Progression.**—Instead of touching a partner, a stick or other article may be carried and transferred, not thrown, from man to man.

Common Faults.

(1) Not waiting to be touched by a partner, or not waiting to receive the stick, &c., before starting.

(2) Standing in front of, instead of "toeing," the line.

3. THREE DEEP.

(a) **Formation.**—Players pair. One pair will be told off as "Chaser" and "Runner." Remaining pairs form a double ring, one man standing behind the other, with at least 2 yards between pairs who face the centre of the ring.

Method of Playing.—"Chaser" and "Runner" take up their positions just outside the ring at opposite points of it. On the word "Go," the "Chaser" pursues the "Runner" with the object of "touching" him. If he succeeds, "Chaser" becomes "Runner," and *vice versa*. "Runner" can take refuge by placing himself, facing inwards, in front of a pair, whereupon the rear man of this pair, now three deep, immediately takes up the role of "Runner."

(b) **Progression.**

Formation.—As above, except that the men of each pair face one another about one yard apart.

Method of Playing.—As above, except that the "Runner" takes refuge *between* a pair, when the one to whom he turns his back becomes "Runner," and the late "Runner" steps back into his place.

This form of the game requires continual alertness on the part of both men in each pair.

Common Faults.

(1) The "Runner" dodges about too long before taking refuge, thus making the game tedious for the others.

(2) In (*a*) the "Chaser" and "Runner" dodge between the two men forming a pair. This is often due to the outer man not standing close enough to the inner one.

(3) The ring is allowed to grow too small. This is bound to occur unless each pair is careful to step back a short pace to its proper relative position in the ring every time a "Runner" halts in front of it.

4. "UNDER PASSING" RELAY RACE.

Apparatus.—Two or more objects about the size of a croquet ball, *i.e.*, balls made out of rags or paper, boxing gloves, &c.

Formation.—Players are formed into two or more ranks (according to numbers of men and balls available), facing the flank.

Method of Playing.—All the players, excepting the last one of each row, stand with their feet at least 3 foot-lengths apart, bend forward from the hips and grasp the hips or belt of the man in front.

The leading player of each row holds the ball; the rear one bends down in a position of readiness to receive it.

At the word "Go," the leading man throws the ball, or other object, backwards to the rear man, between his own legs and those of the other players in his row. The ball should be thrown so as to skim the ground. Should it not reach the rear man in one throw, the nearest player must seize it and pass it on in the same way. As soon as the rear man receives it, he must run to the front of his row and go through the same procedure as No. 1, and so on until the last man gets it, *i.e.*, the original leader. The latter races to the front and places the ball on the ground in front of his feet; the first rank to do this is declared the winner.

Should the ball go outside the players' legs, the player at that spot must fetch it, return to his place and pass it on as described.

Common Faults.

The ball is thrown to the side or too high, instead of straight and skimming the ground.

5. "PLACING THE INDIAN CLUB" RELAY RACE.

(*a*) **Apparatus.**—Two or more Indian Clubs or some similar objects.

Formation.—As in "Under Passing" Relay Race. Opposite, and at about 15 and 20 yards respectively from the front man of each row, two circles of about

8 inches diameter are marked on the ground, one straight behind the other. In the nearest of each of the circles an Indian Club or other object is placed standing on end.

Method of Playing.—At the word "Go," the first player of each row races to the first circle, seizes the club with the left (right) hand, and with the same hand stands it up in the second circle situated 5 yards off. He then races back and touches the outstretched hand of the next man of his row. The latter then races to the club and in the same way places it back in the near circle, and so on alternately until each man of the row has had his turn. The last man, having deposited the club in the circle, races back to the line which the front men were originally "toeing." The first row to finish are of course the winners. Each man, after having touched the outstretched hand of the "next to run," places himself at the rear of his row, which keeps moving forward so that the "next to run" is always "toeing" the original line.

Should the club fall over, the player responsible must replace it in position before the game may be continued.

(*b*) **Progression.**—Between the front man and the nearest circle of each row (which distances should be increased in this case to almost double) a circle of about 1 to 2 yards diameter is drawn.
Each player must, on his way to the club, run round this circle from left to right, and on his way back from right to left. Procedure otherwise as already described.

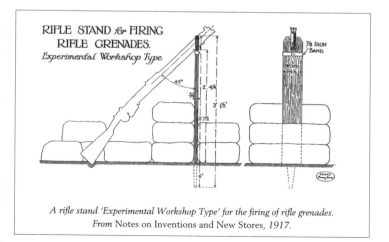

A rifle stand 'Experimental Workshop Type' for the firing of rifle grenades.
From Notes on Inventions and New Stores, *1917.*

Common Faults.

(1) Using both hands or the wrong one to place the club.

(2) Players overstepping the line before being touched by the returning man.

(3) Running round the circles in the wrong direction.

6. "WHIP TO THE GAP."

Apparatus.—A knotted handkerchief, towel or other suitable object.

Formation.—The players stand in a ring at close intervals, lean forward, look on the ground in front of them, and hold their hands behind their backs.

Method of Playing.—The Instructor walks or runs round the outside of the ring and as secretly as possible places the handkerchief in the hands of one of the players. The latter at once chases his right (left) hand neighbour, beating him with the handkerchief as he runs round the ring back to his place.

Both then take their places in the ring and the Instructor proceeds again as before.

The latter should endeavour to deceive the players as much as possible as to whom the handkerchief has been given.

Common Faults.

Players looking round to see who receives the handkerchief.

7.—CHANGING PLACES.

Formation.—All the players but one stand in a circle of about 7 yards or more diameter, facing inward. The odd player stands in the middle.

Method of Playing.—Each player is given a number, which he retains all through the game. The Instructor calls out two numbers (but not, of course, that of the player in the middle), and the players so numbered must change places in the circle. While they are doing so the odd player must try to get into one of the vacated places first, and if he is successful the ousted player then becomes the odd man in the centre.

8.—CIRCLE TOUCH BALL.

Apparatus.—A football.

Formation.—Players stand in a circle 1 to 2 paces apart, facing inward, with one player inside the circle.

Method of Playing.—The football is passed, by hand, from one player to another, and the player inside the circle endeavours to intercept it. If successful, he changes places with the last thrower. If the ball falls to the ground, the player responsible either for the bad pass or missed catch—at the discretion of the Instructor—changes places with the player inside the circle.

Common Faults.

(1) The ball is held too long before passing (about 3 seconds may be put as a time limit for holding the ball).

(2) The ball is kicked, which is wrong, and spoils the whole idea of the game.

9. MAZE.

Formation.—All the players, except two, stand in parallel ranks one behind the other. The distance between each player and each rank is that of "double arm's length," so that whichever direction the ranks may face with arms extended horizontally a line of players with finger tips touching will be formed. The ranks should be drawn up so as to form a square as nearly as possible.

Method of Playing.—The chaser has to pursue the runner up and down the lines until he catches him, neither being permitted to pass under the outstretched arms. The Instructor makes sudden changes in the lines by calling out "Right turn" or "Left turn," on which all turn in the required direction, still keeping the arms outstretched. These sudden changes alter the direction of the paths down which the two players may run. The interest depends greatly upon the judgment of the Instructor in giving the commands "Right (or Left) turn." They should be given frequently and sharply, and often just at the moment when the chaser is about to catch the runner.

The game continues until the runner is caught or a time limit reached, when a new chaser and runner are selected.

Common Faults.

(1) Chaser or runner passing under outstretched arms.

(2) Not changing the chaser and runner sufficiently often.

10. BOMB-BALL.

A game for bringing into play the muscles used in bombing, and for the development of quick and accurate throwing.

Ground.—Any football ground or open space, marked out as under; the size of the rectangle may be varied to suit the amount of ground available.

The goal should be marked out on the ground, no goal-posts being necessary.

Teams.—The players should be disposed as in Association Football, but a lesser number than eleven a side should take part if the ground be small.

Apparatus.—Some object approximating to the weight, size and shape of a grenade, care being taken that it is not such as to be likely to injure the players. The following is suggested:—a small oval-shaped bag of canvas or thick calico, filled with sand or small shot to the required weight and securely sewn up.

Referee.—A referee should control the game, as in football.

Method of Playing.—The ball is passed from player to player by hand, the object being to land it in the goal. It may be passed backward or forward as in Association Football, and the "off-side" rule will apply in the same way. The passes are taken on the run, and the ball must not be held but passed on immediately. If dropped, the ball must be picked up and similarly passed on at once.

The ball may be caught with both hands, but must only be thrown by one. Only two methods of throwing are allowed: (1) For long distances, a full over-hand throw, as shown in the diagrams in "Training and Employment of Bombers," March, 1916; (2) For short distances, a "put," made in the same manner as "putting-the-shot."

In order to exercise equally both sides of the body and to develop skill and accuracy with both hands, the throwing-hand may be changed every 10 minutes or so, at the discretion of the Referee.

To start the game, Captains toss, and the winner has the first throw and the right to select the goal he wishes to defend. The teams are then drawn up, the forwards along their respective starting-lines. The referee blows his whistle and the game commences by the centre-forward taking the first throw or "put."

Rifle Bomb, No. 24, Mark II.
Scale ⅓.
PLATE IX.

The 'No. 24 Mark II' rifle grenade: one of many types of bomb designed to be projected from the rifle.

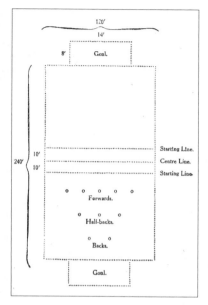

In the course of the game, if the ball lands in the goal, or is caught in the goal, and subsequently dropped within it by any player, a goal is scored.

If the ball is caught in the goal before touching the ground and thrown out at once no goal is scored.

If the ball goes "behind" or into "touch," it is thrown in similarly as in Association Football, but with one hand, and this also applies to a "corner."

After a goal has been scored, the game is started again as at the commencement.

Charging.—No charging or rough play is admissible. Passes may be intercepted, or throws frustrated, with the open hand.

Fouls.—Fouls may be given for (1) Running with the ball, instead of passing it at once as soon as caught or picked up; (2) Throwing the ball in any way but the two methods allowed; (3) Catching hold of a player; (4) Any form of rough play; (5) Being "off-side"; (6) Using the wrong hand for throwing.

Penalties.—A penalty for a foul will take the form of a free throw against the offending side from the place where the foul occurred. In the case of rough play, a goal may be allowed against the offending team for each similar offence after the first caution.

Duration of Game.—From 20 to 30 minutes each way, according to the condition of the men.

CHAPTER 9

Collection of Information Regarding the Enemy, 1915–17

General Headquarters require at all times early and complete information regarding the enemy's units with which our troops are engaged.

Such information is best obtained by:—

(a) A copy of the marks on the identity disc. (This is the most reliable means of identification.)

(b) The pay-book (*Soldbuch*), which has a brown paper cover.

(c) Letters, diaries, and papers found on German soldiers.

(d) The shoulder strap marked with regimental number or monogram. (When shoulder straps are forwarded, it should be stated whether they were taken from a tunic or a greatcoat.)

(e) Markings on arms, clothing and equipment. (The number of the regiment is marked on the inside of the flap of the cartridge pouch and on the bayonet near the hilt. It is also stencilled on the tunic lining and inside the cap.)

The German soldier usually carries all his papers in the skirt pocket at the back of his tunic. Prisoners should be searched as soon as possible after they are captured, to prevent them destroying documents in their possession.

All letters, papers, diaries, pay-books, maps, sketches, messages, operation orders, etc., will be forwarded at once to Divisional Headquarters, with a statement as to when and where obtained, and whether from prisoners or dead (an estimate of date of death is useful if it can be accurately gauged).

Disciplinary action will be taken against any individual found in improper possession of any captured documents.

The fuzes of exploded German shells furnish information required by the artillery. They should be sent at once to the nearest artillery unit with a statement as to when and where they were found.

Exceptions to the above are fuzes marked H.Z. 05 and K.Z. 11. These are **dangerous** even when they have partially exploded and are found separated from the shell.

G.H.Q., "I,"
October, 1915.

CHAPTER 10

Instructions for the Training of Platoons for Offensive Action, 1917.

Issued by the General Staff.

INTRODUCTION.

The Instructions herewith are *in extenso* of those contained in Section IV., para. 5 of S.S. 135, "Instructions for the Training of Divisions for Offensive Action," and must be read in conjunction therewith.

In the last-mentioned document it is laid down, as a result of recent experience, that the Platoon is the Unit in the Assault.

The organisation of a Platoon has been decided in G.H.Q. letter O.B./1919, dated 7th February, 1917. The guiding principles of this organisation are that the Platoon shall consist of a combination of all the weapons with which the Infantry are now armed, and that specialist commanders for Infantry are undesirable.

In O.B./1919/T, dated 14th February, 1917 (S.S. 144), a normal formation for the attack, of which the Platoon is the Unit, has been laid down. The adoption of a normal formation for the attack has been necessitated partly by the shortness of the time which is available for training, and partly by the lack of experience among subordinate commanders.

This pamphlet has been drawn up with a view to assisting Platoon Commanders in training and fighting their Platoons. It is not possible to lay down a correct line of action for all situations which may arise on the battlefield, but it is hoped that a careful study of the instructions herein contained may assist subordinate commanders to act correctly in any situation.

The terms "Trench-to-Trench Attack" and "Attack in Open Warfare" are used in this pamphlet to differentiate from an instructional point of view between the methodical attack of highly organised defences and such attacks as may occur at a later period of an offensive after the main system of the enemy's defences has been penetrated.

It cannot be too thoroughly recognised that although it may be necessary to slightly vary the preparations and form of assembly for the attack in these two sets of circumstances, the actual tactics to be employed will usually be identical.

PART I.

ORGANISATION AND TACTICS.

1. Organisation of a Platoon.

The Platoon is the smallest unit in the field which comprises all the weapons with which the Infantry soldier is armed. It has a minimum strength, exclusive of its Headquarters, of 28 O.R. and a maximum of 44 O.R. If the strength falls below the minimum the platoon ceases to be workable, and the necessary numbers will be obtained by the temporary amalgamation of Companies, Platoons or Sections under Battalion arrangements.

Taking an average strength in the Sections of 36 O.R., a suitable organisation would be as follows:—

		Total O.R.
Headquarters ...	1 Officer and 4 O.R.	= 4
1 Section Bombers ...	1 N.C.O. and 8 O.R. (includes 2 Bayonet men and 2 throwers)	= 9
1 Section Lewis Gunners	1 N.C.O. and 8 O.R. (includes Nos. 1 and 2)	= 9
1 Section Riflemen ...	1 N.C.O. and 8 O.R. (picked shots, scouts, picked bayonet fighters)	= 9
1 Section Rifle Bombers	1 N.C.O. and 8 O.R. (includes 4 Bomb Firers)	= 9
		36

Every N.C.O. and man should carry a rifle and fix his bayonet for the assault, except Nos. 1 and 2 of Lewis Gun and Rifle Bombers if using a cup attachment.

2. Parade.

The Platoon should parade in line, sections at two paces interval, or in Column of Sections; Commanders should be two paces in front of their sections.

3. Ammunition, Bombs, etc., and How Carried.

In each section enough ammunition and bombs can be carried for immediate requirements.

In the trench-to-trench attack, every man (except Bombers, Signallers, Scouts, Runners and Lewis Gunners, who carry 50 rounds) carries at least 120 rounds S.A.A., and 2 or more bombs.

The Lewis Gun Section carries 30 drums (a good method is two haversacks joined with slings or braces, one on chest—two drums, one on back—three drums).

In bombing sections each thrower carries 5 bombs, and the remainder 10 or more each.

Every man in a rifle bomb section can carry at least 6 rifle bombs (a good method is a haversack carried on the back with six or more holes punched in the bottom to take the stick, canvas being attached to the haversack in shape of a bag to protect the sticks).

Flares must be distributed throughout Sections.

Two P. Bombs should be carried by each "Mopper up" in addition to other descriptions.

Any further requirements in S.A.A., Bombs, etc., etc., must be met by carrying parties from other Companies specially detailed.

In open warfare the number of bombs to be carried in the Section of Bombers and rifle bombs in Rifle Bomb Sections may be regulated according to the objectives to be attacked.

4. Characteristics and Uses of the Various Weapons.

(*a*) The rifle and bayonet, being the most efficient offensive weapons of the soldier, are for assault, for repelling attack or for obtaining superiority of fire. Every N.C.O. and man in the platoon must be proficient in their use.

(*b*) The bomb is the second weapon of every N.C.O. and man, and is used either for dislodging the enemy from behind cover or killing him below ground.

(*c*) The rifle bomb is the "howitzer" of the Infantry and used to dislodge the enemy from behind cover and to obtain superiority of fire by driving him underground.

(*d*) The Lewis Gun is the weapon of opportunity. Its chief uses are to kill the enemy above ground and to obtain superiority of fire. Its mobility and the small target it and its team present render it peculiarly suitable for working round an enemy's flank or for guarding one's own flank.

5. The Normal Formations for Platoons and Companies in the Attack.

A. *Trench-to-Trench Attack.*

The Platoon.—

Appendix I. shows a platoon in 1st and 2nd waves.

Appendix II. shows a platoon in Artillery Formation of sections. These can move in fours, file or single file, according to the ground and other factors. Platoon H.Q. should move with that Column best situated for purposes of Command; this will usually be the rear section.

The Company.—   *Appendix III.* shows the normal formation of a Company in two waves, in which the formation of the platoon remains the same.

B. *Open Warfare.*—   *Appendix IV.*

The formations may conveniently be the same as the above when deployment first takes place. The first wave becomes the Firing Line, the second wave the Supports.

"Moppers up" will not usually be required.

6. Working and Carrying Parties.

Working and carrying parties should be detailed by complete sections under their leaders, irrespective of the weapon with which they are armed. They should never be found by detailing a certain number of men from the platoon.

A Platoon acting as a carrying party should move in file, the Sergeant at the head with the guide, the Platoon Commander bringing up the rear. The pace at the head should be slow and Section Commanders must pass down word if they cannot keep up.

When a Platoon is detailed for a working party, its Commander, and no one else, is responsible for the quality and quantity of work performed; he cannot take too much interest in this matter.

7. Tactics of a Platoon in Attack.

In either a Trench-to-Trench attack or in Open Warfare, these resolve themselves in the majority of cases into the method of attack of Tactical Points.

A tactical point may be described as a locality, the possession of which is of first importance locally to either side. It may take the form of any of the following:—

A "strong point," the junction of a communication trench, a cross roads, a bank, a hedge, a house, or other locality of limited dimensions.

The tactics to be employed may be summarized as follows:—

(i.) Push on to the objective at all costs and get in with the bayonet.

(ii.) If held up, obtain superiority of fire and envelope one or both flanks.

(iii.) If reinforcing another platoon which is held up, help to obtain superiority of fire and envelope a flank.

(iv.) Co-operate with platoons on either flank.

For purposes of instruction these may be considered under A.—Trench-to-Trench Attack; B.—Attack in Open Warfare.

A. Trench-to-Trench Attack.—Appendices VIII. and IX.

In regard to:—

(i.) No further comment is necessary, other than to lay stress on the point that waves must go direct *above ground* to their objective.

(ii.) The action of the various sections and Commanders should be as follows:—

> The section of riflemen should, without halting, gain a position on a flank from which to attack both with fire and with the bayonet.
>
> The section of bombers should, without halting, gain a position on a flank and attack under cover of the bombardment of rifle bombs.
>
> The section of rifle bombers should open a hurricane bombardment on the point of resistance from the nearest cover available.
>
> The section of Lewis gunners should in the first instance open traversing fire on the point of resistance from the nearest cover available. At a later stage it may be desirable to work round a flank.
>
> Section Commanders control and lead their sections, keeping touch with the Platoon Commander.
>
> The Platoon Commander controls and directs the sections and sends back information to the Company Commander.

(iii.) One of the most important factors in the action of a platoon reinforcing another is that of its Commander. He should make himself acquainted with the situation before he commits his platoon to any line of action. This is called the personal reconnaissance of the Commander.

(iv.) The means to be employed in Co-operation depend so greatly upon the circumstances at the moment that it is impossible to lay down a definite line of action to adopt. Co-operation means help. If a neighbouring platoon is held up one of the surest ways of helping it is to push on. Touch must always be maintained; this can be effected by means of a patrol of two men, as well as by signal.

B. Attack in Open Warfare.—Appendices X. to XIII.

The line of action described above will usually be found suitable. Owing to the more extended field of action, however, the use of scouts and the personal reconnaissance of the Platoon Commander become of increased importance.

Great opportunities will also occur for mutual support from rifles or Lewis guns for the movement of neighbouring sections and platoons.

8. The Tactics of the Platoon in Defence.

In both Trench and Open Warfare the action to be taken in the defence is practically the same, namely, to hold ground by occupying mutually supporting tactical points, so situated as to be screened from artillery fire, and to obtain:—

(i.) **Observation.**

(ii.) **Field of fire for all rifles.**

(iii.) **Enfilade fire for the Lewis Gun.**

For these purposes the analogy between Trench and Open Warfare is not far to seek. For instance, in occupying a captured position:—

"Consolidation" in Trench Warfare corresponds to the occupation of an "Outpost Position" in Open Warfare.

"Observation Posts" in Trench Warfare corresponds to "Sentry Groups" in Open Warfare.

"Strong Points" in Trench Warfare corresponds to "Picquets" in Open Warfare.

In both cases the necessity for visiting and reconnoitring patrols is equally important.

9. General Rules as to Tactics.

In regard to all tactical situations on the battlefield, the old principles are applicable both to trench warfare and to open warfare and should become a second nature or sub-conscious habit. They may be summarised as follows:—

(i.) *Aim at surprise*, *i.e.*, see without being seen. Do not let bayonets show over the parapet, and take care the assembly is not given away by perceptible movement.

(ii.) *Reconnoitre before movement*. That is to say, work by "BOUNDS," making ground good with scouts before advancing to it.

(iii.) *Protection*. Never remain halted on the field of battle without a look-out. Sentries must be posted, no matter what troops are supposed to be in front.

(iv.) *The Flanks*. (*a*) Guard your own flanks and keep touch with neighbouring units; (*b*) try and get the enemy's flank. For example:—(*a*) In Trench Warfare, Bombing and Lewis Gun Sections guard the outer flank and liaison is kept with neighbouring units; in Open Warfare, scouts must always be employed on an outer flank, one section, usually the Lewis Gun Section, must be told off to act in that direction if necessary, and touch must always be kept with troops on either flank. (*b*) Employ enveloping tactics.

(v.) *Send information back to your Company Commander*. Negative information is as important as positive. You cannot expect assistance from your superiors or from the Artillery unless you tell them where you are and how you are situated.

(vi.) *Hold what you gain*. Never withdraw from a position without being ordered to do so. If where you are is unhealthy and appears untenable owing to casualties, any attempt at withdrawal—anyhow in daylight—will end in increased casualties. Therefore, stay where you are and send back information.

PART II.

TRAINING.

1. To obtain uniformity of ideas and tactics it is necessary for the method to be followed in training platoons to be laid down on broad lines.

2. THE REQUIREMENTS TO BE ATTAINED ARE:—

(*a*) *The Offensive Spirit*. All ranks must be taught that their aim and object is to come to close quarters with the enemy as quickly as possible so as to be able to use the bayonet. This must become a second nature.

(*b*) *Initiative*. The matter of control by even Company leaders on the battlefield is now so difficult that the smaller formations, *i.e.*, platoon and section commanders must be trained to take the necessary action on their own initiative, without waiting for orders.

(*c*) *Confidence in Weapons*, necessitating a high standard of skill at arms.

(*d*) *Co-operation of Weapons* is essential on the battlefield, and is the corollary of (*c*).

(*e*) *Discipline* is most necessary at all times, and particularly on the battlefield.

(*f*) *Moral* must be heightened by every possible means; confidence in leaders and weapons goes a long way towards it.

(*g*) *Esprit de Corps*. True soldierly spirit must be built up in Sections and Platoons. Each section should consider itself the best section in the platoon, and the platoon the best in the battalion.

3. THE METHOD OF ATTAINING THESE REQUIREMENTS

is as follows:—

(i.) The Platoon Commander should divide the time allotted to him for training into two periods, the first being devoted to individual and section training and the second to collective or platoon training and tactical exercises.

(ii.) Training should be progressive, beginning with section drill without arms, saluting, etc., etc., working up to battle formations and tactical exercises.

(iii.) A refresher course every evening for section leaders, in which the next day's work should be gone through, is essential; if they are shaky in it they should practice it then and there.

(iv.) A high standard of skill at arms can only be produced by both the Platoon Commander and Platoon Serjeant being proficient in the use of and able to impart instruction in all the weapons with which the platoon is armed.

(v.) Soldierly spirit in the Platoon and Sections is obtained by encouraging Section leaders to take a pride in their sections and in their work. The formation adopted in falling in on platoon parades tends to bring this about.

Section leaders should inspect their sections before the Platoon Commander inspects the platoon, and they should report them correct or otherwise. At evening entertainments and lectures, Regimental History and accounts of skill at arms and feats of daring on the battlefield should be given prominence.

All ranks must be trained in the following:—

(vi.) Steady drill and ceremonial are necessary to inculcate discipline, of which cleanliness, smartness and steadiness are the bedrock.

(vi.) [sic] Bayonet fighting produces lust for blood; much may be accomplished in billets in wet weather, as well as out of doors on fine days.

(viii.) Bomb throwing and duties of Moppers up require practice and careful study. Moppers up should work in pairs under their own Commander. They drop into their objective and work laterally outwards. They kill any enemy met with in the trenches and guard the entrances to dugouts and side trenches. They must not penetrate down into the dugouts before the platoon for which they are mopping up arrives.

(ix.) Musketry; too much stress cannot be laid on practising the standard tests laid down in Musketry Regulations. These can be practised in billets on wet days just as well as out of doors. Tripods and aim correctors are easily improvised. Good bolt manipulation produced chiefly by the application of the standard tests in the barrack room on wet days, kept the enemy out of our trenches at the beginning of the War, when such luxuries as wire entanglements were not forthcoming. Ranges also are easily improvised.

(x.) Physical fitness:—Route marching, physical training and recreational training, such as football, paper-chases, etc., etc. These latter are best carried out on Wednesday and Saturday afternoons, which, if training is progressing satisfactorily, may be half-holidays.

(xi.) Fire discipline.

(xii.) Wiring.

(xiii.) Field works and filing on tasks. The placing of frames for mined dug-outs may suitably be included in Platoon Training.

(xiv.) Work in the field. Tactical exercises in which the use of ground and choice of cover in both trench and open warfare must receive close attention, are most necessary. An intelligent use of ground frequently enables forward movement to be made without loss. In choice of cover, as a general rule, anything marked on a map or very well defined should, if possible, be avoided to obviate casualties from shell fire. Such exercises can be carried out as a rule within a few hundred yards of billets; it is seldom necessary to waste time by going too far afield, except when route marching and march discipline is being practised. Schemes should comprise the attack of tactical points in trench and open warfare, the action of a platoon, as Vanguard to an Advance Guard, an outpost picquet, etc., etc. The Platoon Sergeant and Section Commanders can be usefully trained by this means when the men are otherwise employed: it enhances their powers of initiative.

(xv.) Gas drill, including bombing, bayonet fighting, and musketry with masks or box respirators on.

Sections must be exercised in their particular weapon:—

(xvi.) The Bombing Section in bombing attack.

(xvii.) The Rifle Bombing Section in quickly forming a rifle bomb bombardment or barrage.

(xviii.) The Lewis Gun Section in coming into action and opening fire quickly.

(xix.) The Rifle Section. The training of this Section is very important. Each man should be a marksman, first class with bayonet and bomb, and a scout, in addition to being either a Lewis Gunner or Rifle Bomber.

Training in certain other subjects is necessary for certain individuals:—

(xx.) Section Commanders. Fire control and description of targets, map reading, observation and information. Salient points in writing messages. Simple tactical exercises.

(xxi.) Scouts and Snipers. Map reading, observation, information and salient points in writing messages and use of appliances. Each section should produce a pair.

(xxii.) Runners and Despatch Carriers. How to find an individual and how to deliver a message.

Certain training must be practised by night as well as day, namely:—

(xxiii.) Bayonet fighting, Bomb throwing, Lewis Gun firing, Musketry, Wiring, Running and Despatch carrying, and Tactical exercises.

(xxiv.) Live Ammunition. No form of instruction with arms can be considered complete until it has been carried out with live ammunition under conditions as nearly as possible approaching those which would pertain on the battlefield.

(xxv.) Competitions. Each form of instruction should be made the subject of a competition, from saluting and clean turn-out up to musketry, accuracy of rifle bombs, scouting, sniping, etc., etc. Prizes are seldom necessary for such competitions, if the result is published in Battalion Orders.

(xxvi.) Thoroughness. As regards dress and arrangements generally, no part of the training should be perfunctory, that is to say, nothing should be left to the imagination; work must always be based on the actual ground and situation as they exist. The turn out should always be in fighting order, with haversacks properly packed and with the full complement of arms and ammunition which would be carried in battle.

PART III.

GENERAL REMARKS.

A Platoon Commander will have gone a long way towards having a well-trained platoon if he has gained the confidence of his N.C.O.s and the men and has established a high soldierly spirit in all ranks.

The confidence of his men can be gained by:—

(*a*) Being the best man at arms in the platoon, or trying to be so;

(*b*) Being quick to act, taking real command on all occasions, issuing clear orders, and not forgetting to see them carried out;

(*c*) Example, being himself well turned out, punctual, and cheery, even under adverse circumstances;

(*d*) Enforcing strict discipline at all times. This must be a willing discipline, not a sulky one. Be just, but do not be soft—men despise softness.

(*e*) Recognising a good effort, even if it is not really successful. A word of praise when deserved produces better results than incessant fault-finding;

(*f*) Looking after his men's comfort before his own and never sparing himself;

(*g*) Demanding a high standard on all occasions, and never resting content with what he takes over, be it on the battlefield or in billets. Everything is capable of improvement from information on the battlefield down to latrines and washing places in billets;

(*h*) Being blood-thirsty, and for ever thinking how to kill the enemy, and helping his men to do so.

The Platoon Commander should be the proudest man in the Army. He is the Commander of *the* unit in the attack. He is the only Commander who can know intimately the character and capabilities of each man under him. He can, if he is so disposed, establish an esprit de platoon which will be hard to equal in any other formation.

A design for dummy 'Chinese Attack' figures. Raised and lowered on the battlefield at the vital moment, these were intended to deceive the enemy that they were under assault, and thus force them to open fire, revealing their positions.

APPENDIX I.

THE PLATOON

Taking an average strength of 36 and H.Q. 4.

(Showing 2 Platoons in 2 Waves, with the right the outer flank).

FORMATION FOR TRENCH TO TRENCH ATTACK.

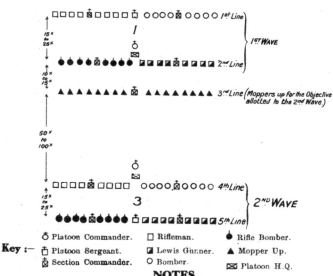

Key :—

♂ Platoon Commander.	□ Rifleman.	● Rifle Bomber.
♂ Platoon Sergeant.	◪ Lewis Gunner.	▲ Mopper Up.
⊠ Section Commander.	○ Bomber.	⊠ Platoon H.Q.

NOTES.

Two Platoons are depicted showing the different positions of leaders in first and second waves.

The Platoon is the unit in the assault, moves in One Wave of two lines and has one definite objective.

Every man is a rifleman and a bomber, and in the assault, with the exception of the No. 1 of Lewis Gun, fixes his bayonet. Men in rifle sections must be trained either to the Lewis Gun or Rifle Bomb.

Bombing and Lewis Gun Sections are on the outer flank of Platoons.

In assembly the distance between lines and waves may conveniently be reduced to lessen the danger of rear waves being caught in enemy barrage, the distance being increased when the advance takes place.

"Moppers up" follow the second line of a wave and precede the unit for which they are to mop up. If the numbers are large they must be found from a different Company or Battalion. Small numbers are preferably found from the unit for which they are to mop up. They must carry a distinctive badge and have their own Commander. G.S.

(12605)Wt. W. 16056-9527 SPL. 44M. 3·17. H & J., Ld.　　　　O.B. No. 1919/T

APPENDIX II.

THE PLATOON
IN ARTILLERY FORMATION
WITH THE RIGHT THE OUTER FLANK.

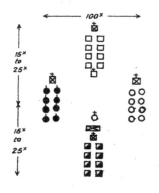

— KEY —

○̇ *Platoon Commander*

☐̇ *Platoon Sergeant*

⊠̇ *Section Commander*

☐ *Rifleman*

◪ *Lewis Gunner*

○ *Bomber*

⊠ *Platoon H.Q.*

● *Rifle Bomber.*

NOTES.

Sections move in fours, file, or single file, according to the ground and other factors of the case.

Platoon H.Q. moves with that column best suited for purposes of command.

APPENDIX III.

THE COMPANY

Taking 4 average strength Platoons of 36 O.R. and Coy H.Q. 14.

FORMATION FOR TRENCH TO TRENCH ATTACK

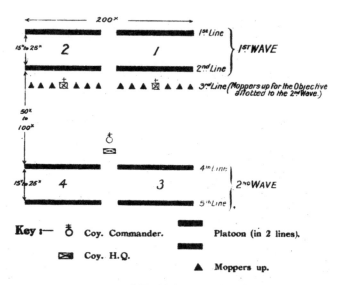

NOTES.

The Company moves in two waves, has two objectives and is distributed in depth.

"Moppers up" follow the second line of a wave and precede the unit for which they are to mop up. If the numbers are large they must be found from a different Company or Battalion. Small numbers are preferably found from the unit for which they are to mop up. They must carry a distinctive badge and have their own Commander.

G.S.
O.B. No. 1919/T

APPENDIX IV

THE PLATOON

Taking an average strength of 36 and H.Q. 4.

(Showing 2 Platoons in 2 Lines with the right the outer flank).

FORMATION FOR ATTACK IN OPEN WARFARE.

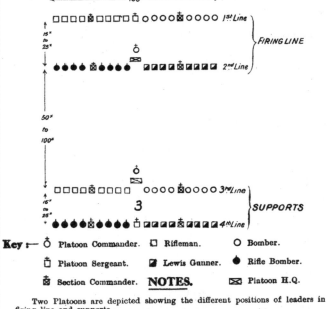

Key :— ☐ Platoon Commander.   ☐ Rifleman.   ○ Bomber.

☐ Platoon Sergeant.   ☐ Lewis Gunner.   ● Rifle Bomber.

☐ Section Commander.   **NOTES.**   ☐ Platoon H.Q.

Two Platoons are depicted showing the different positions of leaders in firing line and supports.

The Platoon is the unit, has one definite objective, and can move in two lines as above or form one line as circumstances dictate. Two lines are most easily obtained from artillery formation.

Every man is a rifleman and a bomber, and in the assault, with the exception of the No. 1 of Lewis Gun, fixes his bayonet. Men in rifle sections must be trained either to the Lewis Gun or Rifle Bomb.

Bombing and Lewis Gun Sections are on the outer flank of Platoons.

The number of bombs and rifle grenades to be carried will be decided by the nature of the objective distance to be traversed and other considerations.

G.S.
O.B. No. 1919

APPENDIX V.

Suggested daily programme during Summer months:—

FIRST PERIOD.

Before Breakfast.
Section Drill.

After Breakfast.
One hour each section in its own weapon, the rifle sections being allotted half to the Lewis Gun Section and half to the Rifle Bomb Section.

One hour the whole platoon bomb throwing.

One hour physical training and bayonet fighting.

Finish the morning with ceremonial, that is to say, form up and march past the Platoon or Company Commander on the way to dinners.

After Dinners.
Communicating drill and control of fire drill. Musketry on the range alternately by sections.

Recreation at 4 p.m.

N.C.O.s refreshed in the next day's work at 6.30 p.m.

APPENDIX VI.

SECOND PERIOD.

Before Breakfast.
Platoon drill.

After Breakfast.
Half hour whole platoon bomb throwing.

One hour instruction in wiring, digging, and filing on tasks; scouts and snipers—information, map reading and message writing; runners and despatch carriers; moppers up.

One hour physical and bayonet training.

Last half hour. Fire control and fire discipline.

Ceremonial on the way to dinners.

After Dinners.
Simple tactical schemes.

Recreation at 4 p.m.

N.C.O.s refreshed in the next day's work at 6.30 p.m.

Simple tactical schemes.

NOTE TO SUGGESTED PROGRAMME.

For examples of exercises in the field both in Trench-to-Trench Attack and in Open Warfare see Appendices VII. to XIII.

If training is progressing satisfactorily half-holidays should be allowed on Wednesdays and Saturdays.

Men who prove themselves efficient should be excused certain parades. Individual keenness is easily promoted and easily rewarded.

During Winter months work should not begin till after breakfasts, *e.g.*, at 8.30 a.m. The half-holidays are of greater importance than during the Summer because on other days there is not sufficient light after 4 p.m. for games.

Smoking Concerts and Lectures should be given on Wednesday and Saturday evenings.

APPENDIX VII.

EXAMPLES OF USEFUL EXERCISES IN OPEN WARFARE.

1. Advance or Flank Guard schemes.—The Platoon finding the advance parties, is held up by a tactical point, necessitating a fight. (*See* Appendices X and XII.)

Points to be watched:—

(i.) **The use of ground and scouts.**

(ii.) **The correct use of weapons.**

(iii.) **The plan should be that of enveloping tactics.**

2. Outpost schemes.—This should involve the placing of each individual on the actual ground. For instance, Sentry Groups, the Sentry over the Picquet, reliefs for visiting and reconnoitring patrols, deciding what points are to be held, and how they are to be held in event of attack, the placing of the Lewis Gun.

3. A tactical point is encountered with a machine gun. Tactics of the supporting Platoon. Particular attention should be paid to the personal reconnaissance of the Commander to the use of ground and weapons, and to the plan which should be of the nature of enveloping tactics. (*See* Appendices VIII., IX., X., and XII.)

4. *Village Fighting.* In this the Lewis Gun can be employed to keep down the enemy's rifle fire while bayonet men and bombers bound down the *right hand* side of the street, clearing house by house. It is always better, if possible, to enter a house from the back rather than the front.

5. *Wood fighting.* A line of skirmishes who fire while advancing (*v.* para. 8 of S.S. 135, "Instructions for the Training of Divisions for Offensive Action") followed by Sections in small columns has been found a convenient formation. Much attention to keeping direction is necessary.

APPENDIX VIII.

TRENCH TO TRENCH ATTACK

PLATOON IN 1st WAVE
MEETING A POINT OF RESISTANCE.

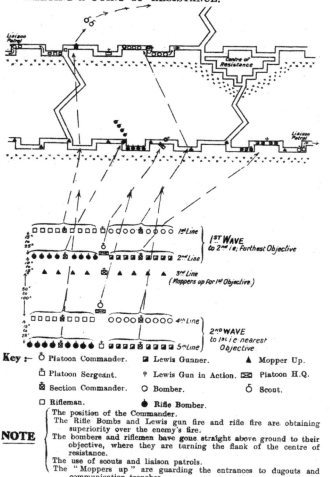

Key :—

Ò Platoon Commander.	◼ Lewis Gunner.	▲ Mopper Up.
⌶ Platoon Sergeant.	✝ Lewis Gun in Action.	⊠ Platoon H.Q.
⊠ Section Commander.	O Bomber.	Ò Scout.
☐ Rifleman.	● Rifle Bomber.	

NOTE

{
The position of the Commander.

The Rifle Bombs and Lewis gun fire and rifle fire are obtaining superiority over the enemy's fire.

The bombers and riflemen have gone straight above ground to their objective, where they are turning the flank of the centre of resistance.

The use of scouts and liaison patrols.

The "Moppers up" are guarding the entrances to dugouts and communication trenches.
}

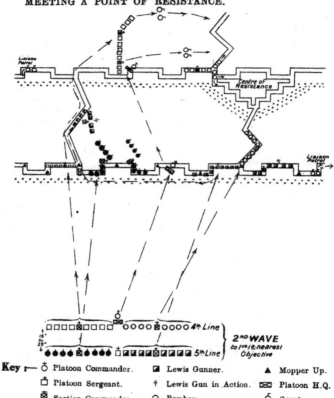

APPENDIX IX.

TRENCH TO TRENCH ATTACK

PLATOON IN 2ND WAVE
MEETING A POINT OF RESISTANCE.

Key :—   ȯ Platoon Commander.   ◪ Lewis Gunner.   ▲ Mopper Up.

ᗡ Platoon Sergeant.   ✝ Lewis Gun in Action.   ⊠ Platoon H.Q.

⊠ Section Commander.   O Bomber.   ȯ Scout.

□ Rifleman.   ● Rifle Bomber.

NOTE.   The Commander of 2nd Wave gets in touch with the situation on reaching his objective through the Commander of his Moppers Up and the Commander of the 1st Wave. He then decides to help the 1st Wave, the Commander of which goes on to his own objective.

NOTE, especially in the action of the various sections, the attack above ground.

APPENDIX X.

ATTACK IN OPEN WARFARE
CORRECT METHOD OF ACTION OF A PLATOON IN FIRING LINE, MEETING A POINT OF RESISTANCE.

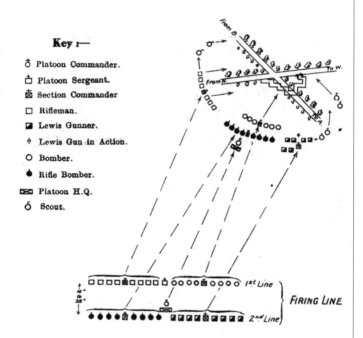

Key :—

Ƌ Platoon Commander.
⌂ Platoon Sergeant.
☒ Section Commander
☐ Rifleman.
▰ Lewis Gunner.
ɸ Lewis Gun in Action.
○ Bomber.
● Rifle Bomber.
▱ Platoon H.Q.
Ƌ Scout.

NOTE.

Correct use of scouts. Sections are under the hands of their Commanders. A firing line has been built up, rifle bombs, Lewis gun fire and rifle fire are being used to obtain superiority over enemy fire. A flank is being turned.

APPENDIX XI.

ATTACK IN OPEN WARFARE
INCORRECT METHOD OF A PLATOON IN FIRING LINE, MEETING A POINT OF RESISTANCE.

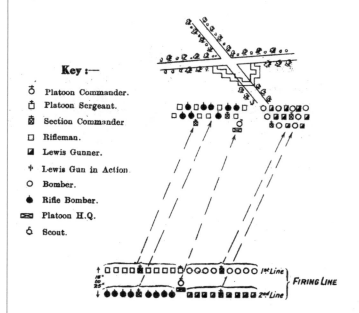

Key :—

ŏ Platoon Commander.

ḃ Platoon Sergeant.

⊠ Section Commander

☐ Rifleman.

◪ Lewis Gunner.

⊹ Lewis Gun in Action.

○ Bomber.

● Rifle Bomber.

⋈ Platoon H.Q.

ŏ Scout.

NOTE.

No scouts are employed. Sections are mixed up and not under the hands of their Commanders. No firing line has been built up. No attempt at enveloping tactics is being made.

APPENDIX XII.

OPEN WARFARE

CORRECT METHOD OF ACTION OF A PLATOON IN SUPPORT.

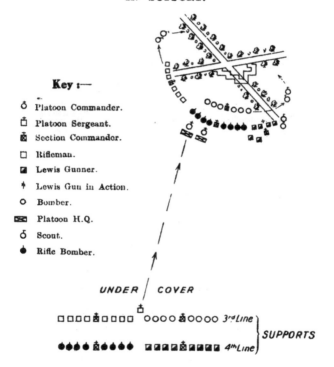

Key :—

ŏ Platoon Commander.

⌷ Platoon Sergeant.

⌷ Section Commander.

□ Rifleman.

◪ Lewis Gunner.

⸸ Lewis Gun in Action.

○ Bomber.

▧ Platoon H.Q.

ŏ Scout.

● Rifle Bomber.

UNDER | COVER

□ □ □ □ ▧ □ □ □ □   ○ ○ ○ ○ ▧ ○ ○ ○ ○ *3rd Line*

● ● ● ● ▧ ● ● ● ●   ◪ ◪ ◪ ◪ ▧ ◪ ◪ ◪ ◪ *4th Line*

SUPPORTS

NOTE.

The Platoon Commander is seen making his personal reconnaissance some hundred yards ahead, with the Platoon waiting under cover under Platoon Sergeant. On result of this reconnaissance he can act on either flank, dependant on the ground and the situation.

APPENDIX XIII.

OPEN WARFARE

INCORRECT METHOD OF ACTION OF A PLATOON IN SUPPORT.

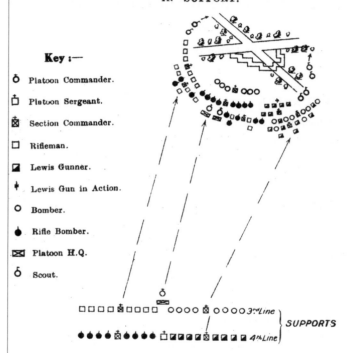

Key :—

ŏ   Platoon Commander.

ḋ   Platoon Sergeant.

⊠   Section Commander.

□   Rifleman.

◪   Lewis Gunner.

⸍   Lewis Gun in Action.

O   Bomber.

●   Rifle Bomber.

⊠   Platoon H.Q.

ŏ   Scout.

3rd Line
4th Line   } SUPPORTS

NOTE.

The Platoon Commander of the Supports is shown as having led his Platoon right up to the Platoon already engaged, where it arrives in confusion. He has made no personal reconnaissance and is committed to one flank only. This line of action could only be adopted where good cover exists immediately in rear of Platoon engaged, in which case even, the Platoon Commander should have gone ahead and finished his personal reconnaissance by the time his Platoon arrives.

CHAPTER 11

Gas Warfare.
Monthly Summary of Information.

No. 15.

Issued by the General Staff, September, 1918.

I.—OFFENSIVE.

I.—Operations of the Special Brigade, R.E.

During the month of September, 63 operations took place on 20 nights, a total of 294 tons of gas being discharged at the enemy by means of projectors and Stokes mortars. In addition, smoke and oil were successfully employed on several occasions.

General.—The following extracts from an order issued by the Seventeenth German Army in July, 1918, show the effectiveness of the gas operations recently carried out by the British on the Arras front.

"Owing to the severe losses we have suffered and to the impossibility of providing our troops with a more convenient form of protection, the army command is obliged to resort to energetic measures.

"Close investigation regarding recent projector attacks and the casualties incurred has furnished the following data:—

"(*a*) The enemy carries out his projector attacks during the period from two hours after sunset to one hour before dawn, a time when atmospheric conditions are particularly favourable for the use of gas.

"(*b*) The forward zone, which is the target area of projector bombardments, is full of activity at this time; ration parties are coming up, reliefs are taking place and working parties are busy.

"(*c*) The concealment of the projector attack by means of heavy H.E. and machine gun fire makes it difficult to recognise the flash and deto-nation; the adjustment of the mask, therefore, does not take place in time.

"As regards (*a*), on nights when a gas attack is imminent, *i.e.*, on all nights when it is neither raining heavily nor blowing hard, a special gas alert will be ordered. All gas-proof curtains will be lowered and special sentries will take up their positions at the dug-out entrances.

"As regards (*b*), all ration and working parties will, on such nights, continue the last 1000 yards of their journey to the front line with the mask adjusted. The extension will be put on, if a thick cloud of gas is encountered.

"As regards (*c*), the mask will be adjusted on principle, at every burst of artillery fire, as latterly the enemy has rarely employed H.E. shell alone.

"Although it must be admitted that losses are unavoidable owing to the heavy concentration of gas produced in the case of direct hits, yet the majority of the casualties are shown, by the reports of units, to be due to surprise and carelessness."

Evidence of results not previously known.—On the 6th July, 1918, projector drums were fired on to the enemy's positions E. of Meteren. The results of the operations are indicated by the following extract from a captured order, dated 13-7-18, issued by a neighbouring division:—

"A hostile projector attack, recently carried out against a neighbouring sector, caused considerable casualties."

A captured German intelligence summary of the 233rd Div. gave the following information concerning casualties inflicted by a projector and Stokes mortar shoot near BEAUMONT-HAMEL, on the 13th July, 1918:—

"Very heavy artillery and machine gun fire was suddenly opened on the 13th July, at 12.45 a.m. At 1 a.m., the enemy made a strong surprise projector attack opposite the left flank of the 30th R.I.R., causing rather heavy losses. This again shows that the enemy is trying to conceal his gas projector attacks in every possible way and that only extreme alertness can save us from suffering heavy casualties."

On the 20th and 21st July, 1918, two small Stokes mortar and projector bombardments were carried out near Dernancourt and Albert, a sector occupied by the 54th Res. Div. A captured order of this division, dated 22-7-18, states:—

"On the 20th and 21st July, the division suffered no small losses from hostile gas projector attacks. In both cases the enemy masked his attack by artillery fire. Every H.E. bombardment by the enemy is, therefore, to be looked upon as a gas alarm and masks are to be adjusted accordingly."

A projector operation on the 4th August, 1918, near Colincamps, inflicted about 100 casualties on the 1st Battn., 184th I.R.

The following account of a projector bombardment shows the value of the employment of gas in connection with operations. On the night of the 9th/10th August, 1918, a small number of projector drums were fired against Mural Farm, a strong point in the vicinity of Meteren. On the night of the 21st/22nd August, a number of dummy drums were fired against the same strong point and an infantry assault was carried out three minutes later. The objective was taken and 22 prisoners and 2 machine guns captured with very slight loss. The British division, on whose front the assault took place, issued the following report:—

> "Mural Farm was held by the 88th I.R., 56th Div. Prisoners of this regiment were captured there. A prisoner of the 88th I.R., examined as to the results of our projector shoot on the 9th/10th August, stated that one company had 20 gas casualties including 6 who died 5 or 6 hours after the gas attack; three other companies had 10–15 casualties each. Such prisoners as were captured were found with their masks on and there is no doubt that the ease with which the objectives were taken was due in large part to the dummy projector operation."

Projector and Stokes mortar operations on the 4th and 5th August, 1918, in the Hulluch sector, killed 27 men in the 2nd Coy., 371st I.R.

The success of a projector attack, made on the 13th August, 1918, against the 234th Div. near Moyenneville, is shown by the following extract from a captured German order of the neighbouring division, the 2nd Gd. Res. Div.:—

> "The rather heavy losses suffered by the neighbouring division on the right render it necessary again to call attention to the danger of projector attacks."

Confirmatory Evidence.—The effective results of British cylinder discharges during August and September, 1916, in the Armentieres sector, have been confirmed by a captured German document dated November, 1916, belonging to the Gas Officer of the Sixth German Army:—

> "Considerable losses were caused by the gas attacks which have taken place latterly. The casualties were mainly due to the men being surprised in dug-outs, to the neglect of gas discipline, masks not being at hand, to faulty masks and to the use of old pattern drums which could not afford protection against the type of gas employed by the enemy."

A captured order of the Fourth German Army, dated 13-6-18, furnishes information regarding the gas losses of the 12th Div. in the Merris sector during May, 1918. (*See* "Gas Warfare," Nos. 11, 12 and 14, May, June and August, 1918,—total gas casualties of this division during May, 1918, over 200, including many dead). The following is an extract from the above Army order:—

On the night of the 23rd/24th May, shortly after midnight, the British carried out a heavy surprise bombardment with H.E. ammunition (shell and bombs) on the positions occupied by the 12th Inf. Div. west of Merris. *At the same time*, a projector attack was made with phosgene drums. The area bombarded included the positions of three regiments on a front of 1,500 metres and a depth of 400 metres. The target is thickly scattered with exploded drums, as many as 900 being counted afterwards.

"The enemy carried out here for the first time a variation of his earlier tactics, as he did *not* carry out separate H.E. and gas bombardments, following one another in rapid succession, but projected gas drums *during* the H.E. bombardment.

"The recognition of the nature of the bombardment was made extraordinarily difficult for the troops. The garrison was taking cover and only a few of them noticed the bright flash of the projector discharge, while the report of the exploding drums was lost in the noise of the bursting shell and H.E. bombs. For the same reasons, the noise of the drums in the air remained unnoticed.

"Even though the British have so often violated the technical laws of gas warfare as regards wind conditions on other occasions, it is still surprising that they should have carried out a gas projector attack on the night in question. There was a very steady south-west wind, with a speed of 13 miles per hour or more, blowing towards the British line.

"The gas cloud was certainly very dense immediately after the attack. It was well on the target, as a large part of the trenches received direct hits. However, the cloud was rapidly dispersed by the high wind.

Losses.

11 men killed (certainly on account of the gas attack).

121 men gassed (including 2 officers).

In addition, 16 men died afterwards during treatment.

"To the credit of the troops it must be emphasized that their good gas discipline and their skill in the use of their masks under adverse conditions enabled them to avoid *even greater losses*."

After a small projector shoot near Meteren on the 6th July 1918, 29 bodies of men who had been killed by gas were found in the target sector. (Compare "Gas Warfare," No. 13, July 1918—gas casualties of the enemy regiment holding this sector amounted, during June, to 5% of its strength).

THIS EXCELLENT
THRASHING MACHINE

FOR SALE,

As Owner has no further use for it. He had it made to his own design in 1914 to be used in thrashing the Allies. Further comment is absolutely unnecessary.

—o—o—o—

APPLICATIONS DIRECT TO OWNER :—

K. A. ISER,

"The Retreat,"
Amer de Hollande,
Holland.

SOME PRESENT DAY WAR RIBBONS

1st Series

V.C. ARMY

DIST. SERVICE MEDAL

DIST. SERVICE MEDAL
INDIA

ALBERT MEDAL IN GOLD
SEA

ALBERT MEDAL (SEA)

DIST. SERVICE ORDER

DIST. CONDUCT MEDAL

ALBERT MEDAL IN GOLD
LAND

ALBERT MEDAL (LAND)

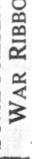

V.C. NAVY

DIST. SERVICE CROSS
CONSP. GAL. MEDAL (NAVY)

MILITARY CROSS

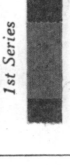

MILITARY MEDAL

NAVAL GEN. SERVICE

2.—Gas Shell.

The following account illustrating the harassing effect of our gas shell has been captured:—

"From 2nd Bttn. to 15th Inf. Regt. 30.7.18.

Report concerning gas cases.

A company was moving up in groups into position when gas was noticed during the march near Morcourt. Gas masks were immediately brought into the alert position and put on. It was supposed that the enemy would cease firing gas shell after a short while, but this proved to be wrong, rendering it necessary to continue the journey through the gas. The last group had two cases of rifle grenades to carry and this was a very laborious task considering that masks had to be worn at the same time.

Men removed masks at times when they thought that the gas had disappeared. As a result of this continued removal and adjustment of the mask, the men must have breathed a certain amount of gas. Just in front of Lamotte, they came into a thick gas cloud so suddenly that it was not possible to adjust the mask in time. Owing to these conditions, the company had 8 men gassed."

A prisoner of the 5th Bty., 1st Foot Art. Regt., stated that during our recent gas bombardment of Bourlon Wood, all batteries in and near the wood sustained gas casualties, the most serious being those of the 6th Bty. which had 45 casualties although they wore masks adjusted. This battery (21-cm. howitzer) had not been able to fire for 10 days on account of the position being "flooded with gas." The other batteries were able to carry on under difficulties. He stated that the gas used on the night of the 25th/26th September went through their masks and caused casualties. The prisoner was intelligent and reliable, and had been used by his battery for forward observation.

The following information has been obtained regarding the first of our B.B. bombardments on the night of the 26th/27th September on the Fourth Army front:—

A stretcher bearer belonging to the 8th Div., captured on the 30th September, said that he saw 80 gas casualties passing through Vendhuille aid post on the morning of the 27th. The men belonged to the 153rd I.R. and 72nd I.R.

The occurrence of heavy gas casualties in this area from a gas which was described as smelling of garlic or onions was also confirmed by 5 prisoners of the 3rd Bn., 153rd I.R. Rations failed to reach the troops on two occasions owing to ration parties being gassed. The 3rd Bn. suffered gas casualties estimated at 25% of its strength.

The 11th Coy. alone lost 20 to 30 men. One prisoner stated that men did not wear their masks and took no precautions against the gas.

In the Bellenglise sector, a N.C.O. of the 263rd R.I.R. stated that he had been told that 30 gas casualties had been caused in his regiment. A group of officers were asked if any of them had been in our gas bombardment, and an artillery officer said, with emphasis, that it was "sehr schlimm" (very bad). They subsequently became suspicious and refused to answer any more questions. The officer was severely censured afterwards by the others for giving away information about gas.

A man of the 28th R.I.R. (185th Div.), who was obviously himself suffering from the effects of the gas (hoarseness, cough and eye inflammation), said that no one in his company wore masks and that subsequently at least 9 or 10 men went sick. Stretcher bearers of the same regiment confirmed this.

Reports from our own artillery indicate that many enemy batteries were neutralized, in some cases remaining silent for the whole of the next day.

A large number of the prisoners examined, especially stretcher bearers and medical orderlies, knew of the occurrence of small numbers of casualties (two or three at a time) and it seems that there was a steady dribble of gas cases from many units during the morning of the 27th.

3.—Enemy's Defensive Measures and Appliances.

(a) *Information from captured documents.*

The great number of enemy documents on gas defence captured during recent operations shews that he has been much harassed by our gas attacks. The number of similar documents issued by our Allies and ourselves is small in comparison with the number of enemy publications.

Organization.—A summary of the organization of the German Gas Services appears in one document, which states that the command of the Gas Service in the field is vested in the "Commander of the Gas Troops" (*Kommandeur der Gastruppen*) at General Headquarters. This officer was formerly known as the "Inspector of Gas Regiments."

Gas questions are dealt with by the Chemical Section (*A 10*) of the War Ministry and instruction in gas warfare is centralized at the Army Gas School (*Heeres-Gasschule*) in Berlin. Experimental work is carried out at the Kaiser Wilhelm Institute for Physics and Electro-Chemistry, at Berlin-Dahlem.

There is an Anti-Gas Inspectorate (*Kgl. Inspektion des Gasschutzdienstes für das Heimat-Gebiet*) and a main Anti-gas Depot (*Hauptgasschutzlager*) in Berlin.

As far as is known, the only technical troops employed in gas warfare are the 35th, 36th, 37th, and 38th Pioneer Battalions.

Protection.—The enemy has issued orders broadcast to the effect that every heavy H.E. bombardment is to be considered as a gas alarm, and gas masks are to be put on.

Such an order appears under the signature of the 54th (Württemberg) Res. divisional commander and is dated 22nd July.

An important document issued by the 222nd Inf. Div., dated 8-7-18, (translation received from A.E.F.) deals with conduct during hostile bombardments.

"Artillery Orders.

"When a battery is bombarded with gas shell for a relatively long period, the battery commander, if the tactical situation permits, will evacuate the position temporarily and report the fact to the sub-group. Some one will remain at the telephone, but telephonic communication from the gas-proof dug-out will be established with the least possible delay.

"The gunners must be withdrawn from the danger zone. They will, however, remain sufficiently near, so that it will be possible to open fire quickly (wearing masks) in case of necessity (barrage fire, etc.). Watch must be kept for signals requesting barrage fire, etc.

"The sub-group will allot the tasks of the battery in question to other batteries as far as possible.

"If the situation does not permit the evacuation of the position (*e.g.*, if the battery has important missions to fulfil, as happened to the 8th Battery of the 278th Regiment), all men not indispensable will be kept in gas-proof dug-outs. The position will be evacuated as soon as the tactical situation permits.

"In the case of night bombardment with Yperite shell, the position will be evacuated again at daybreak even if the effects of the gas are not perceptible, because the gas becomes noxious under the action of the sun's rays."

An order of the 225th Div., dated 2-7-18, states that, in future, 6 to 8 oxygen breathing sets will be held by each company for use in the event of our using new gases.

The gas officer of the above division, in a minute dated 6-8-18, addressed to the Long-Range Group Gas Officer, ordered that all old rubber breathing tubes with fixed mouth-pieces which would not screw into the mask were to be exchanged at the Anti-Gas Depot at Framerville. Batteries were to report by August 13th and 18th, that all *Selbstretter* (mine rescue sets) were fitted with new tubes which rendered possible the combination of the *Selbstretter* with the gas mask.

Another document of the 16th Inf. Div., dated 7-6-18, contains orders for the distribution of a gas alarm. In the case of ordinary gas shoots by night, the alarm is only given locally. For heavy artillery gas bombardments or projector attacks, the alarm is spread "locally" by the artillery, but "generally" by infantry commanders and telephone operators, the direction of travel of the cloud being mentioned if possible.

Training.—The following is a syllabus of the course of instruction at the Gas School at Berlin:—

1. "Royal Prussian Army Gas School.
Berlin N.W. 40. Invalidenstr. 55a.

| Scheme of work | | 8–13/4/18. |
| Section I. | | Instructor Major Fromm. |

Monday.

9.30–9.45	General instructions	Major Fromm.
9.45–10.45	Introduction to gas warfare	" "
11.00–12.15	Cloud gas and projectors	Lt. Westphal.
12.15–1.00	Gassing of areas	Lt. Schwarz.

Tuesday.

9.30–10.15	Enemy gas warfare material	Major Fromm
10.30–12.15	Artillery gas bombardments	" "
12.30–1.30	The U-boat war	Kapt. z. S. v Mantey.

Wednesday.

9.30–10.15	First aid for gas casualties	O. Arzt Falkenberg.
10.15–11.00	Meteorological service at the front	Lt. Schwarz.
11.15–12.15	Gas projectors	Hptm. Thorner.
12.30–1.00	Protection of animals	Lt. Vet. Bauer.

Thursday.

		Major Fromm,
9.0–9.30	Practical work	Lt. Schwarz.
		Lt. Runne.
9.30–10.45	Basis of gas defence	Major Fromm.
11.00–11.45	Oxygen apparatus	" "
11.50–12.50	Attitude towards enemy gas attacks	Lt. Schwarz
12.50–1.30	Testing of masks in gas chamber	–

Friday.

Gas work in the open.

Instructor—*Rittmeister* Frh. v Gersewald.

(Times will be definitely intimated later.)

Saturday.

9.30–10.15	Gas Services in the Field and in the Home territory	Major Fromm.
10.30–11.30	Final discussion	
11.30–12.30	Aviation tactics	Major Siegert.

(Sd.) Oberst Goslich."

(*b*). *Enemy defensive organization in areas recently captured by us.*

It is now possible to form an idea of the development of enemy defensive organization since 1917.

General.—A comparison of the recently captured area with the Hindenburg line captured in November, 1917, shows that the enemy has developed his gas defensive measures considerably since that date. Except in certain sectors, little attention is paid to collective protection, but the supply of respirators, drums, oxygen sets, etc., is well organized. The provision of all anti-gas appliances appears to be in the hands of the Gas Services.

Individual Protection.—In addition to the appliances described in "Gas Warfare," No. 14, August, 1918, p. 9, several respirators consisting of an ordinary drum with a flexible tube and mouthpiece without facepiece or goggles (*see* "Gas Warfare," April, p. 6) were found in battery positions, so they appear to be used by gunners or artillery personnel in addition to aviators.

Many specimens of the "*A.W. Feldprüfer*" for testing the resistance of drums were found. These are not issued to formations but two are kept at each anti-gas store.

Every store also contained large numbers of the small oxygen breathing sets (*Selbstretter*) though the large ones (*Heeres-Sauerstoff-Apparat*) were not so common. Several large oxygen cylinders and pumps for filling the small oxygen bottles from them were found.

The enemy appears to make great use of these oxygen sets, for they have been found littered about battery positions and headquarters all over the area; the large number of spares, returned empties and spare potash cylinders in the stores also confirms this view.

Collective Protection.

Dug-outs.—The thoroughness with which the gas-proofing of dug-outs was carried out varied greatly with the formations. For example, prisoners of the 2nd Guard Res. Div. had stated that their gas discipline was good; this was borne out by an examination of the area which they held. They had fitted woven paper fabric curtains or blankets to the entrances of their mined dug-outs according to our method, which they had obviously copied. The angles at which the curtains were set varied from vertical to 60° from the vertical, but they were in many cases badly fitted. Signal wires, stove pipes, etc., frequently passed between the battens and the curtains.

In other large areas, dug-outs for the most part had no protection at all, even mine shafts and tunnel entrances having no curtains in spite of the numerous orders issued on the subject.

In a very few cases, dug-outs were found protected at a distance of 10,000 yards from the line.

In the entrances to most of the dug-outs opposite our Third Army front, about 10 lbs of chloride of lime were kept stored in a box.

Alarms and gas zones.

Gas alarms were installed at the entrances of practically all dug-outs. These alarms consisted of British 18-pr. cartridge cases, iron wheels or rails with strikers, bells and large flat metal discs with strikers. Farther back, there were Klaxons, hooters and sirens.

The sirens, which are very effective, are of two sizes, and each type consists of a centrifugal fan rotated at high speed by means of a handle and gear wheels. In the larger type, the fan rotates within a casing perforated round its circumference by 16 rectangular slots. The 16 vanes of the fan on rotation draw in air, and this is forced through the corresponding slots, which are rapidly opened and closed by the flat ends of the vane, thus giving the siren effect. The weight of the larger type is 26 lbs, of the smaller 18½ lbs.

There appeared to be no continuous chain of alarms, although the importance of this has been recognised, as shown by the following divisional order of the 109th Inf. Div., dated 14-5-18:—

> "The importance of the gas alarm must be repeatedly pointed out. Since the breakdown of the telephone in connection with the front line troops is always possible, the communication of the gas alarm to the rear can only be assured by the use of loud sounding alarm apparatus."

No portable alarms, such as our rattles, were found in the captured territory.

Notices defining gas zones were found opposite our Second Army front. The danger zone was about 10,000 yards, and the alert zone about 5,000 yards behind the front.

(c). Enemy medical organization for dealing with gas casualties.

It is clear from captured documents dealing with the medical aspects of gas poisoning that the Germans have suffered a considerable number of severe casualties from gas, as well as fatal cases. Instances of the prejudicial effect of muscular exertion after phosgene poisoning and of the occurrence of severe or fatal delayed cases, are frequently given.

Gas casualty stations, with specially trained personnel, have now been established in Army areas, so as to deal with cases showing definite symptoms of gas poisoning, since "experienced medical officers, and, in particular, a thoroughly trained male and female nursing staff alone render it possible to do justice to individual gas cases and to attain favourable results." (Instructions issued in May, 1918, *i.e.*, before the Germans had been shelled with Mustard Gas).

The experience is quoted of one of these gas stations which treated 70 severe cases of phosgene poisoning, and of another which dealt with 658 mustard gas cases in July.

Difficulty has been experienced in dealing with malingerers or alleged cases of gas poisoning, and instructions have been issued that such cases are to be held up in the medical inspection rooms of their units, or of bearer companies, with a view to returning them direct to duty in 24 to 48 hours, if no objective symptoms develop. This difficulty is emphasized in an order of the 1st Res. Div. which suffered 215 gas casualties between the 21st and 31st August when it was in line opposite the French. There was a strong suspicion in this case that some men had either feigned gas sickness or wilfully exposed themselves to gas with a view to escaping duty, and men were to be instructed that they would be tried by court-martial in such cases.

II.—DEFENSIVE.

1. Enemy Cloud Gas.—No attacks reported.

2. Enemy Projectors.

Several more enemy projector positions have been found, and captured orders indicate that others were about to be prepared. All projectors found on our front have been of the smooth bore type, though some on the American and French fronts have been of the rifled type.

Further details are now available for addition to the accounts given in "Gas Warfare," No. 14, August, 1918, pp. 13 and 14.

18-cm. (smooth bore) projector.—The emplacements were in parallel rows, well camouflaged with the usual German woven paper fabric, dry vegetation being placed on top to assist in screening. Air photographs, however, showed these positions distinctly, as well as the tracks leading to them.

In one position, 123 projectors were found, and in another, over 200. The angle of elevation varied from 30° to 45°; possibly the enemy varies his range by altering the elevation instead of the charge.

The fuzes used were *Z.s.u.m.W.M.* and in one position were set for 23 seconds, though the percussion arrangement was free to act.

For a description of the bomb, *see* para 3 (iii.) below.

16-cm. (rifled) projector.—Reports from the French show that this projector fires an 80-lb. bomb (H.E. or gas) to a range of at least 3,300 yards.

The projectors were found spaced about 2 feet apart (centre to centre) in trenches. About 5% of those that had been fired had burst. The leads are carried up the bore, passing through grooves in the rifling of the bomb.

In the middle of July, the enemy was experimenting with the following methods of setting up the projectors:—

(*a*) The projector buried up to the muzzle, no base plate being used.
(*b*) The projector set up on a base plate placed at the bottom of a trench about 2½ feet deep, with the muzzle resting on the spoil thrown up in front of the trench.

(c) The base plate placed on the ground and the muzzle of the projector supported by a wooden framework.

For a description of the bombs, *see* para 3 (iii.) below.

3. Gas Shell and Trench Mortar Bombs.

(i.) *Enemy's tactics.—Captured documents and prisoners' statements.*

(a) "Hours for firing Yellow Cross gas shell," C.G.S. of the Field Army, II, No. 93949, dated 7-8-18:—

"Bombardments with Yellow Cross shell will be executed preferably between 1 a.m. and 4 a.m. At first, the bombardment compels the enemy to wear his mask. A few hours later, when the presence of the gas is no longer revealed by its odour, the enemy will probably take off his mask, and in consequence he will be gassed after sunrise owing to evaporation from the ground. For this reason, the principal lines of resistance of the enemy, chiefly groups of dug-outs, machine gun emplacements and infantry observation posts which have been located, as well as battery positions, should be bombarded with Yellow Cross shell whenever the weather permits.

"Every attempt by the enemy to neutralize the effects of our night gas bombardment in the morning should be prevented by bursts of rifle, machine gun, trench mortar and artillery fire."

(b) Order from the War Ministry, Berlin, circulated by the Gas Staff Officer of First German Army under date 2-3-18:—

"Firing trials with gas shell carried out at Kummersdorf have given the following results:—

At a distance of 1,000 metres from the point of impact and with a wind blowing towards our troops, Green Cross gas clouds are still dangerous to troops without masks, which must therefore be worn. The gas alert must be maintained up to 3,000 metres."

Prisoners of the 27th Foot Art. Regt. stated that the usual rate of fire for gas shell in their (15-cm. howitzer) battery was 1 round per gun per minute. Neither masks or gloves were worn when firing Yellow Cross shell, though they had orders to wash their hands after firing gas shell.

(ii.) *Enemy's activity.*

During the active operations of the month, the enemy made extensive tactical use of gas shell, though he did not get the opportunity of firing trench mortar and projector bombs.

His bombardments, except when carried out in conjunction with operations during the day time, have nearly all taken place at night.

At times he fired large quantities of gas shell in high winds but produced practically no effect.

His use of gas shell may be classified as follows:—

(*a*) *Blue Cross used alone.*—This was used extensively in the preparation for enemy counter-attacks, in the enemy's barrage during our attacks and in scattered harassing fire. There is very little evidence that this gas alone is instrumental in causing an appreciable number of casualties.

The heaviest bombardments of this nature were as follows:—

> Bertincourt–Ytres district, 4,000 rounds on the night of the 4th/5th September. Inchy, 3,000 rounds on the night of the 4th/5th. Batteries near Metz and in Havrincourt Wood, 3,500 rounds on the afternoon of the 19th. On a large area N.E. of Estaires, 3,000 rounds on the 15th.

(*b*) *Green Cross, or mixtures of Green and Blue Cross shell.*—These were mostly of the type of surprise shoots, and were generally employed in frequent heavy bursts. When the *mixture* was used, Blue Cross shell were generally fired first.

Most of these bombardments consisted of small numbers of shell.

The more important shoots were as follows:—

On battery positions near Rumaucourt, 1,500 rounds Green Cross on the early morning of the 11th September.

On other positions near Rumaucourt, 800 rounds Green and Blue Cross at the same time.

N. of Wulverghem, 800 rounds Green and Blue Cross on the night of the 23rd/24th.

Green Cross 3 shell were fired in small bursts at times, but no extensive use of this filling was reported.

(*c*) *Yellow Cross, or mixtures of Yellow and Blue Cross, (sometimes with the addition of a few Green Cross shell).*—As usual the bulk of the gas shelling, except during enemy counter-attacks, is included under this heading.

Several large concentrations of Yellow Cross were fired into back areas, battery positions, and sometimes on to forward systems, generally at a steady rate of fire maintained for several hours.

Forward posts were often engaged in order to render them untenable, and very large concentrations were often used to create an "impassable zone" when our attacks were expected.

The *mixture* was used chiefly during our attacks or on suspected points of assembly, more especially in valleys and hollows.

The more important bombardments of this nature were as follows:—

In the valley of the Canal du Nord, near Manancourt, 1,000 rounds mixed Yellow and Blue Cross on each of the nights of the 3rd/4th, 4th/5th and 5th/6th September, during our attacks across the valley.

In the Buissy valley at various times. This area was under direct observation by day; hence treatment of the ground could not be fully carried out. In spite of this, one of the larger Yellow Cross bombardments produced no casualties.

In the Bouchavesnes and Mt. St. Quentin areas, just after these had been captured.

On the front system near Mericourt, S. of Lens, 10,000 Yellow Cross rounds during the night of the 5th/6th (an attack by us being expected).

In the area Steenwerck—Nieppe—Neuve Eglise, 6,000 rounds Yellow Cross on the night of the 18th/19th, following an attack by us on the previous day, in which we had captured some ground near Ploegsteert.

On battery and other positions in woods, particularly Havrincourt wood, on various occasions.

(iii.) *Enemy chemical shell and bombs.*

Ammunition stocks in a German division.—The following table shows the theoretical and actual stocks of ammunition in the battery positions and in the divisional dump of the 192nd Div. (in line in the Moreuil sector) at the end of July, 1918. The amount on charge, in each case, is an average based on the figures for 3 days:—

A.—In the battery position.

Calibre	Number of batteries.	Average number of rounds per battery.					Establishment per battery.
		H.E.	Blue Cross.	Green Cross.	Yellow Cross.	Total	
Field Artillery—							
7.7-cm. gun, '96 n/A	3	2283	143	118	290	2834	2000
7.7-cm. gun, '16	3	1824	273	99	125	2321	2000
10.5-cm. howitzer	3*	2166	294	170	109	2739	1600
Foot Artillery—							
10-cm. gun	1	1187	399	214	207	2003	1200
15-cm. howitzer	3*	936	200	–	81	1217	1000
21-cm. howitzer	2	560	–	82	121	763	600

B.—*In the divisional dump.*

Calibre	Average number of rounds on charge.				Establishment for dump.			
	H.E.	Blue Cross.	Green Cross.	Yellow Cross.	H.E.	Blue Cross.	Green Cross.	Yellow Cross.
Field Artillery—								
7.7-cm. gun, '96 n/A	4560	1446	576	471	1500	900	900	–
7.7-cm. gun, '16	1577	2026	6143	574	1500	900	900	–
10.5-cm. howitzer	1230	1310	–	50	1200	450	450	–
Foot Artillery—								
10-cm. gun	1005	–	545	234	300	150	150	–
15-cm. howitzer	390	639	437	89	500	152	152	–
21-cm. howitzer	419	–	126	28	300	–	120	–

* Of these, one battery was out at rest.

The battery establishments laid down for this normal active sector should be compared with those given for a defensive battle front on page 95 of "The Handbook of the German Army in War," April, 1918.

Examination of enemy dumps.

(*a*) *Proportion of gas shell.*—In dumps opposite our Third Army front, the proportions of the various shell were about 60% H.E. and shrapnel, 30% Blue Cross, 10% other gas shell. Of the Yellow Cross shell, about 50% were of the H.E. variety.

Opposite our Second Army front, the proportions were about 70% H.E. and shrapnel, 27% Blue Cross and 3% other gas shell.

This points to the great confidence of the enemy in Blue Cross shell.

(*b*) *Storage.*—Gas shell were stored both in the upright position and lying on their sides. As a rule they were kept several yards to the rear of positions, in small pits containing up to 500 rounds and scattered over a wide area. Different types were stored separately, though at times Blue and Green Cross shell were mixed (the enemy often uses this mixture in surprise shoots).

Yellow Cross shell were hardly ever found at battery positions, but appear to have been carried up at the last possible moment before use. At times, they were found stacked on planks over pits. No definite protection from sunlight was noticeable.

(*c*) *Fuzes.*—No Yellow Cross shell were found with time fuzes, indicating that no air bursts were intended, at any rate on the battle front; a few Blue Cross shell, however, were found fitted with time fuzes, possibly by accident. The rods of instantaneous fuzes were not found in forward dumps; these were stored in boxes at the main dumps.

10.5-cm. Blue Cross shell with new filling.—Several shell, identical in all respects with ordinary Blue Cross shell, except for the chemical filling, have been found to contain N-Ethyl Carbazol.

The bottles containing the substance have three crosses etched on the shoulder, and their contents weigh about 336 grammes in each case.

The compositions of the fillings of two shell examined by the Central Laboratory were:—

Diphenylchlorarsine	44 and 55%,	respectively.
N-Ethyl Carbazol	51 and 41%	"
Tarry matter	5 and 4%	"

The French have described other specimens with equal quantities of the first two substances.

N-Ethyl Carbazol is a crystalline substance, of M.P. 68°C. and B.P. 189–191°C. under 15 mm. pressure; it is far less irritating than diphenylchlorarsine (*see* "Gas Warfare" No. 14, Aug. 1918, App. I).

10-cm. gun gas shell.—A large quantity of fixed gas ammunition was found at 10-cm. gun positions, but the shell themselves were in all cases ordinary 10.5-cm. howitzer shell fixed in a gun cartridge case. They are probably fired with a reduced charge.

Variations in Yellow Cross I (Green Cross 3) fillings containing ethyldibromarsine.—A few 10.5-cm. howitzer shell have been examined in which the limits of the composition are somewhat different from those mentioned in "Gas Warfare," No. 14, August, 1918, App. I. The limits for shell containing ethyldibromarsine should read:—

Ethyldichlorarsine	35–60%	
Ethyldibromarsine	16–45%	Density of filling
Dichlormethylether	10–20%	at 15°C. generally
Arsenic chloride	0–5%	about 1.82.
(possibly due to decomposition)		

15-cm. Green Cross (phenylcarbylamine chloride) shell, impurities.—In an unfired shell of type *15 cm. Gr. 12*, painted grey with a green cross on the base, and containing 5,160 grammes of filling, a small amount of solid had been deposited, consisting of 10 grammes of sulphur and 30 grammes of triphenylisocyanurate $(C_6H_5NCO)_3$.

About 1.4% of the filling consisted of chlorphenylcarbylamine chloride.

15-cm. Blue Cross shell, weight of filling.—In a grey *15 cm. Gr. 12* shell, marked with blue bands and blue crosses in the usual manner, the bottle, weighing 0.914 kg., was abnormally large and contained 1.481 kg. of diphenylchlorarsine.

(The usual weight of filling is about 1.0 kg.)

15 cm. H.E. Yellow Cross shell, variations in.—A specimen examined contained the usual quantity (2800 grammes, or 2250 cc.) of the normal Yellow Cross substance with 1230 grammes of H.E. It was a short shell, *15 cm. Gr. 12 verst.*, painted black, with a yellow band from the driving band to the base end, a Lorraine cross on each side and one on the base. The fuze was the *Gr.Z.14 n/A.* Others contained 700 grammes of H.E., separated from the liquid by a plug of cement and by a hemispherical diaphragm of metal. (Add. to Appendix II, "Gas Warfare," No. 14, August, 1918).

21-cm. Green Cross 3 Shell.—(*See* "Gas Warfare" No. 14, Aug., 1918, App II). The French report a shell of the type *21 cm. Gr. 96 n/A.* (modified) fitted with a *Gr.Z.17* fuze. It is painted grey, carries a green cross on its base, and is the first 21-cm. shell yet found containing the Green Cross 3 filling.

Marks as below are cold stamped on the shoulder:—

+	(large size)
+ 3	(small size)

The weights are:—

Empty shell	104.170 kg
Fuze	0.975 "
Liquid contents	15.055 "
	120.200 "

Volume of liquid at 15°C. 9500 cc.

The liquid, which is of a dark colour and of density 1.582 at 15°C., has the composition:—

Dichlormethylether	32%
Ethyldichlorarsine	68%

21-cm. Yellow Cross shell containing nitrobenzene.—Shell of this calibre have now been found to contain the normal Yellow Cross filling with dichlorethylsulphide, nitrobenzene and chlorobenzene (*see* "Gas Warfare," No. 14, Aug., 1918, page 21).

White Cross marking for overweight H.E. shell.—A *15 cm Gr. 12 (verst.)* was found to be an overweight H.E. shell, marked with a white cross on its base to indicate this, the shell being painted black.

7.6-cm. (light) "Minenwerfer" bombs (Green, Yellow and Blue Cross).—*See* "Gas Warfare," August, 1918, App. II).

A drawing captured in a German dug-out was marked "*Bezeichnung der leichten Gas Minen,*" and showed three light *Minenwerfer* bombs marked on their shoulders with a Green, Yellow and Blue cross, respectively. Above the coloured cross, one, two, and three cold stamped crosses were indicated, respectively, and four "G"s were stencilled on the body of each bomb.

Phosgene bombs containing small quantities of carbon tetrachloride and hexachlorethane, examined at the Central Laboratory, were painted grey and these were also marked with four white "G"s. They contained 577 grammes of liquid filling.

18-cm. (smooth bore) projector bomb.—H.E. and phosgene bombs (unfired) have been examined.

The H.E. bomb is painted bluish grey and weighs 27.5 kg. The bursting charge weighs 8.056 kg. and consists mainly of ammonium nitrate mixed with various nitro-bodies. The bomb is intended to be used with the *Z.gl.W.M.* (time) fuze.

The *phosgene* bomb is coloured grey and marked with 3 white bands and the letter "A" stencilled in white. Fuze, *Z.s.u.m.W.M.* (25 secs.).

Weight of bomb	29.167 kg.
Bursting charge	.143 kg. (0.023 kg. in fuze gaine)
Volume of liquid	5,170 cc.

The exploder tube is 85 mm. shorter than in a bomb previously examined, but contains more T.N.T., as there is no wooden block.

The French have examined two 18-cm. projector bombs of the same type fitted with *L.W.M. Zdr.2* fuzes and adapters. The filling in these bombs is phosgene—diphosgene in the proportions 75 to 25 and 57 to 43.

16-cm. (rifled) projector bombs.—The H.E. bomb is made of steel and painted grey with a red 'S' in two places on the shoulder. On the body is painted, in black, "WF1 16" and in white "FULL HAM" with a date. The length (without fuze) is 637 mm., and the weight with fuze 36 kg.

A *phosgene* bomb described by the French (*see* "Gas Warfare," No. 14, Aug., 1918, App. II) has a green cross on the base and on the fuze. The filling consists of small light yellow granules of pumice with liquid phosgene; there is more than enough phosgene to impregnate the pumice as about one litre of liquid can be poured out on emptying the contents.

The object of the pumice granules appears to be to increase the persistence of the phosgene.

Weight of bomb empty	24.000 kg.
" " pumice	2.530 ,,
" " phosgene	6.620 ,,
Total	33.150 kg.

Volume of space for chemical filling 7,700 cc.

Fuze *Z.s.u.m.W.M.*, graduated from 15–45 seconds (instead of from 7–25 seconds).

GLOSSARY

'WAR ESTABLISHMENTS' OF UNITS EXTRACTED FROM THE
FIELD SERVICE POCKET BOOK, 1914.

Infantry Regiment	Variable establishment [A number of battalions united by cap badge, traditions, and recruitment.]
Infantry Battalion	30 officers, 977 other ranks (four companies)
Infantry Company	6 officers, 221 other ranks (four platoons)
Platoon	Each platoon led by an officer, and each platoon comprised four sections each led by a junior 'non commissioned officer' (NCO).
Infantry HQ and MG section	6 officers, 93 men
Cavalry Regiment	26 officers, 523 other ranks
Cavalry Squadron	6 officers, 152 other ranks
18 pdr Field Artillery Brigade	23 officers, 772 other ranks, 18 guns
18 pdr Field Artillery Battery	5 officers, 193 other ranks, 6 guns
4.5 in Howitzer Brigade	22 officers, 733 other ranks, 18 howitzers
4.5 in Howitzer Battery	5 officers, 192 other ranks, 6 howitzers
Heavy Artillery Battery	5 officers, 163 other ranks, 4 guns
6 in Siege Battery	5 officers, 177 other ranks, 4 howitzers
Engineer Field Squadron	7 officers, 184 other ranks
Engineer Field Company	6 officers, 211 other ranks
Divisonal Signal Company	5 officers, 157 other ranks
Field Ambulance	10 officers, 224 other ranks
Cavalry Field Ambulance	6 officers, 118 other ranks
Divisional Supply Train	26 officers, 402 other ranks

Cavalry Brigade	85 officers, 1,633 other ranks
Cavalry Division	439 officers, 8,830 other ranks
Infantry Brigade	124 officers, 3,931 other ranks
Infantry Division	585 officers, 17,488 other ranks

Index

Page references in *italics* refer to illustrations or captions.

Abbeville 6
aircraft 4, 49
  aerial observation 50
  British measures against enemy aircraft 49, 52, 78-79; AA guns 50-51
  coordination with artillery 50
Albert 140
Armentieres 141
Army Ordnance Corps 58
Army Printing and Stationery Services 6-8, 11
Arras front 139
artillery 4, 13, 23, 45, 47, 69, 71, 76, 78, 103, 122
  ammunition 51
    4.5 howitzer 51
    60-pdr 51
    gas 85
    HE shell 50, used to mask gas attacks 139-140, 142
    shrapnel 78
    smoke 85
  tactics 49-51
    attack 14, 15, 18, 20, 50, 86
    barrages 85, 88
    concealment 50
    coordination with aircraft 50
    cutting wire 85, 88
    defence 47, 50
    liaising with infantry 15, 50
    spotters 50
Atteridge, A H 7

barbed wire 47, 60, 68-69, 73, 75, 76, 86, 104, 107
  cutters 80, 87
  manual cutting 86-87, 89
  use of artillery to cut 85, 88
Bates, Montague 7
Beaumont-Hamel 140
Bellinglise 144
Bertincourt-Ytres 152
Bethune 55
bicycles 49, 59
billeting 59-63
bivouac 5
Bostock, Sgt-Maj J 93
Bouchavesnes 153
Boulogne 6
Bourlon Wood 143
British Army
  23rd Division 77
  bombers 11, 67, 72, 74, 118, 121, 125
  drill 9, 123-124, 131-132
  inspections 124
  logistics 56
    equipment and clothing 57-59
    lorries 56
    procedure at railhead 56-57, 58; rendezvous 57; refilling point 57, 58
  machine gunners 67, 100-101; training 91, 100; *Machine Gunner's Handbook 93*
  morale 123
  platoon organisation 118, *127*, 158

removing equipment 54
  relations with civilians 60-62
  sentries 70, 73, 74-76, 82, 122, 132
  signallers 67, 80
  steel helmets 77
  stretcher bearers 75, 80, 88
  training 5, 123-125, 131-132, *133, 134, 135, 136, 137, 138*
    manuals 6-12; *Field Service Pocket Book 5, 5, 9*
  working parties 120
buglers 20
Buissy Valley 153

cavalry 47, 48, 52, 58, 158; reconnaissance 49
Chapman, Guy 8
chemical munitions 4, 7, 11, 66, 85, 87, 88, 98, 139-157
  British attacks with gas 139-144
  British countermeasures 66
    procedure in gas attack 71-72, 125
    Smoke helmets 71
    Vermorel sprayers 69, 72, 78
  British delivery methods 139
    gas shells 143
    Livens projector 139, 140, 141, 142
    Stokes mortars 139, 140, 141
  gas masks 139-142, 143, 144, 146, 147, 148, 151
  German countermeasures 144-150; German Anti-Gas Inspectorate 144; German Anti-gas Depot 144, 145; German Army Gas School 144, syllabus 146-147
    alarms 146, 148-149
    dealing with casualties 146, 149-150
    dug-outs 148
  German delivery methods 150; German field gas forces 145
    16cm rifled projector 150, 157
    18cm smooth bore projector 150, 157
  German Gas Shells 151-157; fuzes 154, 155, 157; stocks 153-154
    Blue Cross shell 152, 153, 154, 155, 156
    Green Cross shell 151, 152, 153 154, 155, 156, 157
    Yellow Cross shell 151, 152, 153, 154, 155, 156
    Minenwerfer 156
  German reports of British attacks 139-142, 143, 144, 149
  types of chemical
    Arsenic Chloride 155
    Carbon tetrachloride 157
    Chlorine 66
    Chlorobenzene 156
    Chlorphenylcarbylamine chloride 155
    Dichlorethylsulphide 156
    Dichlormethylether 155, 156
    Diphenylchlorarsine 155
    Diphosgene 157
    Ethyldibromarsine 155

Ethyldichlorarsine 155, 156
  Hexachlorethane 157
  Mustard 149
  N-Ethyl Carbazol 155
  Nitrobenzine 156
  Phosgene 142, 149, 157
  Sulphur 155
  Triphenylisocyanurate 155
Chinese Attack figures *126*
Colincamps 140
command and control 16, 18
communications 15, 18; carrier pigeons 10, 65
corrugated iron 40

Dane, Edmund 7
Dernacourt 140
derrick *44*
Dressing Stations 45

Espionage 10, 65
Estraires 152

Field Ambulances 48, 59; Mark VI *61*
Field Engineering 22-23, 124
  entrenching tools 51, 59, 69-70
  Gun Emplacements 22, *32*
  Machine Gun Emplacements *33*, 92, 97, 100, 101-102; dugouts 102-103
  Redoubts 22, *38, 41, 42*
  Trenches 9, 15, 22, 30, 31, 35
    bombing posts 69
    design 28
    disguising 28-29
    disposal of earth 28
    drainage 39, 68, 75
    firing step 29
    frozen ground 29
    kitchen *41*
    latrine *41*, 63, *63*
    loopholes 23, 26, 27, 34, 39, 45, 68, 102, 106; steel 39
    machine guns 98-107
    overhead cover 40, 51
    parapets 22, 23, 28-29, 75
    positioning 22, 28, 51-52
    shelters 40, 74
    stockades *43*
    traverses 39-40, 51, 52, 68
    types
      communication 22, 30, 40, 45, 51, 89
      cover 22, 24, 29, 40
      fire 22, 23-29, 23, 24, 36, 37, 40, 51, 52, 79; positioning 23, 28
      support 52, 74-75
field glasses 76, 80
Field Service Regulations 12
Framerville 145

General Staff 60, 62, 84
Germany Army 46
  4th Army 141
  6th Army 141
  17th Army Divisions
    1st Reserve Division 150
    2nd Guard Division 148
    8th Division 143
    12th Division 141-142

16th Infantry Division 146
54th Reserve Division 140
56th Division 141
109th Infantry Division 149
225th Division 145
233rd Division 140
artillery 45, 46, 48, 50, 78;
  accuracy 51; shells 116
ruses 52, 64-65

Havre 6
Havrincourt Wood 152, 153
Hindenburg Line 147
HMSO 5, 6
Hulluch 141

infantry, tactics 4, 122
bombing 55, 68-70, 78, 113, 124;
  training 125, 131
defensive 46, 121
  advance posts 46
  against counter attack 72-73
  protective troops 46
fields of fire 52
formations
  artillery formation 119, *128*
  attack 119-120, *127*
  defence 121-122
  marching 48; discipline 48-49,
    123
  look out post *44*, 45
Minor Enterprises 84-89;
  selection of men 85; training
  86-87; attire 87-88; supports
  88
night operations 48
offensive 12-21, 117-138; object
  12-13
  battalion attack 15-17, 16, 18, 21
  checked 14
  covering fire 13-14, 16, 18
  effect of terrain 13-14, 15, 17,
    19, 20, 21
  final assault 20-21; charge 20
  fire fights 13, 20
  firing line 12, 14, 15, 17-19, 20
  General Reserve 12
  grenadier party attack *72*
  'hasty cover' *21*, 29
  line of advance 12
  local reserves 12, 13, 14, 15, 16,
    17
  pursuit 20-21
  reconnaissance 12, 122
  rounding a traverse *78*
  scouts 12, 17-18, 52, 125;
    training 131
  supports 12
  tactical points 14
  trench to trench 121, *129*, 132,
    133, *134*
  open warfare 121, *130*, *135*, *136*,
    137, *138*
passage of rivers 47
rapid fire 53; training 124
skirmishers 52
snipers 67, 73, 74, 76, 125;
  training 131

machine guns 4, 10, 11, 13, 14, 49,
  69, 90-107, *93*; overview 90-
  93, 104-105
ammunition supply 97, 101
concealment 92, 98, 100, 102,
  106
cooperation with infantry 92-93,
  97, 98, 100
nature of fire 91

ranges 91; range cards 97
tactics
  advance guard 94
  defensive 96, 97, 98-103;
    reserves 96
  offensive 16, 18, 86, 88, 94-96,
    103-104
  open warfare 93-98
  positioning 97-98, 100
  streetfighting 96-97
  suitable targets 91
  trench warfare 98-107
types
  Maxim 102
  Vickers 102
    limbers 96, 97
  loopholes 102
Manancourt 153
maps 54, 79, 94
Mericourt 153
Merris 141-142
Meteren 140, 141, 142
Metz 152
mines 73, 77, 88; mining 75
mirrors 45
Morcourt 143
mortars 4, 76, 88
motorcycles 59
Mt St Quentin 153
Moyenneville 141

Neuve Eglise 153
New Church Times 8, *8*
Nieppe 153
North, Maj E B 10, 83

officers, general remarks 126
billeting 59-62
equipment 58
Non Commissioned Officers 52,
  70, 74, 75, 76, 80, 86, 104,
  118, 119, 126, 131
role in attack 14-21, 117-138; use
  of horse 17
Standing Orders
  daily meetings 73-74
  daily programmes 131
  daily returns 82
  garrisoning trenches 74
  obtaining information 76, 85,
    116
  patrolling 75-76, 84-89
  posting sentries 70
  procedure for prisoners 82, 116
  procedure for relieving troops
    67-70
  reconnaissance 75, 84-85
  reports 68-69
  Standing troops to Arms 70-71
  use of machine guns 93-107
  watches 70
Ordnance Officer 57

Partridge, Capt S G 6
periscopes 69
Ploegsteert 153
Pullman A1 Shield *79*

railway trucks 56
refugees 65
Rheims 65
River Aisne 50, 51, 55
River Mons 10, 55
Royal Army Medical Corps 59, 80
Royal Engineers 5, 6, 14, 47, 59
Royal Field Artillery 56, 59
rubbish disposal 81, 83
rum 10, 75, 83

Rumaucourt 152

sandbags *26*, *27*, 28, 34, 39, 69,
  75, 81
signalling 65, 77, 94, 100; test
  signals 77; SOS signals 77
small arms
  ammunition 14, 17, 18, 19, 23,
    29, 48, 118-119, 125; muddy
    53; supply 55-56, 58; stores
    68-69; storage 75
  bayonet 11, 13, *20*, *20*, 52, 53,
    72, *78*, 86, 87, 118-119, 121-
    124; training 125, 131
  catapults 69
  flamethrowers 4, 87
  grenades *55*, 69, 86, 87, 88, 114,
    119, 124
  grenade throwers 69, 88
  Joubert dagger *81*
  Lewis Gun 10, 11, 88, 90, 94, 97,
    99, 103, 104-107, *104*, 118,
    122, 125
    ammunition 119
    attack 106-107
    training 125, 131, 132
    trench warfare 105-106, 121
    maintenance 53-54
  rifle grenades 7, 69, 88, *111*, *114*,
    119, 121, 124-125; No. 24
    Mark II *114*
  Short Magazine Lee Enfield *20*
  Very Signal Pistol 68, 69, 70, 101
  Webley Mark IV revolver *13*
Solano, E J 7
spies 65
Steenwerck 153
stretchers 28, 51

telephones 69, 79, 88, 100, 149
torches 87
transport 48
trains 49
troops
  care of feet 6, 83
  cooking *9*
  dress 81
  discipline 48, 74, 126
  drunkenness 83
  entertainment 131-132
  food supply 23; tinned rations 80-
    81
  frost bite 63-64
  games 10-11, 108-115, 124
    Bomb-Ball 11, 113-115
    Changing Places 112
    Circle Touch Ball 112-113
    Indian Club relay race 110-112
    Jumping the bag 108
    Maze 113
    Relay race 109
    Three deep 109
    'Under passing' relay race 110
    Whip the Gap 112
  latrines 62, 63, *63*, 80, 83; urine
    tins 63
  messengers 82, 100, 125
  PT 11, 108, 124, 131
  water supply 23, 62-63, 80, 82

weather forecasts 86
wheelbarrow 28
wounded 17; care of 80
Wulverghem 152

Ypres 8, 55

Zeppelins 79